YOU ARE A MEDIUM
(YOU JUST DON'T KNOW IT YET)

Hannah Macintyre

First published in paperback by
Michael Terence Publishing in 2024
www.mtp.agency

Copyright © 2024 Hannah Macintyre

Hannah Macintyre has asserted the right to be identified
as the author of this work in accordance with the
Copyright, Designs and Patents Act 1988

ISBN 9781800947122

All rights reserved. No part of this publication may be reproduced,
stored in a retrieval system, or transmitted,
in any form or by any means, electronic, mechanical,
photocopying, recording or otherwise,
without the prior permission of the publisher

Front cover background image
Copyright © Maria Starovoytova
www.123rf.com

Rear cover Author image
by Shannen Lythgoe
www.shannenlythgoe.co.uk

Cover design
Copyright © 2024 Michael Terence Publishing

Michael Terence
Publishing

To Spirit,

Thank you. For everything x

This book is dedicated to Kate & Jay – sent from spirit exactly when I needed you most! Thank you for your hours of work, cheerleading my weary self into motivation and helping me turn my vision into reality.

This book would not be what it is without you. Not all angels reside in the Spirit world!

Contents

Foreword 1

1: Introduction 2

2: Foundations 16

3: The Spirit World 23

4: Vibration Rising 30

5: I'm Not Good Enough 49

6: Spooky Stuff 56

7: How it Works 69

8: The Psychic Frequency 83

9: The Healing Frequency 93

10: The Spirit Guides Frequency 102

11: The Evidential Mediumship Frequency 120

12: The Trance Frequency 147

13: Taking It Further 152

Acknowledgements 171

Foreword

You're already doing it. You are, you know? You are connecting to Spirit every day, multiple times a day. And that is what makes this so fascinating. For most of us that connection is so understated, so gentle, that it is hard to believe anything is really happening!

This book will help you recognise and understand the connection that you are using all the time. You will learn how to pay attention to that connection, expand it, and believe in it.

Connecting to the Spirit world is available to all humans. The ability is within us, calling us, guiding us. It is so subtle and quiet that we disregard it most of the time; but it does not mean we are unaware of it. Our human focus prioritises information from the physical world. We are conditioned from birth to concentrate on what we can see, smell, touch and understand. Our work, when we decide to try to connect to Spirit, is all about undoing that and learning to trust in something that is completely unquantifiable.

Can you hear that voice in your head piping up with hundreds of reasons why this will never work for you?

That is okay. I have that voice too. It is part of being human.

So much of Spirit work is shrouded in mystery by teachers who want to keep the power for themselves, when in fact it is surprisingly simple. You are already doing it. You are a medium. (You just do not know it yet.)

I
Introduction

"Hannah Macintyre is a phenomenal medium, known for her superb accuracy and great sense of humour. She has wowed audiences around the world with her connection to the Spirit world."

Sounds impressive, right?

If you look at my write-ups on my website or social media you will see something similar to the above. And while I am incredibly proud of my work for Spirit and my achievements so far, it wasn't always like this. In fact, I have found learning mediumship incredibly challenging.

I am the epitome of "getting in your own way." I have over-analysed, doubted, and ripped apart my mediumship so many times. But every time I have fallen, I have picked myself back up and learnt from these experiences. And I cannot help thinking that I am exactly who I was always supposed to be, because this book is the culmination of the knowledge gained from my mistakes and the understanding I have gained from getting it wrong.

I want to start this book by taking you back to one of my first communications with Spirit. I had been sitting in a Spirit guide development group for about a year, and in honesty, was having great results with messages delivered from guides to my fellow students. I could channel an inspirational address at the drop of a hat, and pull a card and wow someone with my message. But there was a large part of me that still did not believe I could actually "do" mediumship. My messages felt too generic. I could not feel or see anything that felt clear enough for the magnitude of this work. Surely if you throw enough proverbial darts at a dartboard, you will hit the target eventually? Where was the proof? Where was the evidence?

My journey was too strange. I had not had what I would call, "a calling." I had rocked up to this group to watch other mediums work, not to do it myself. That is not how callings work – you get a shining effigy at the end of your bed, a Spirit looking somewhat like Gandalf, reading from a scroll about your destiny, right?

Whilst everyone assured me I was doing it right, I still felt wrong. I just did not understand why it was not clearer, tangible, more like what you see on the television.

Mentally chewing over all these thoughts, I was in the kitchen with my friend, Lorraine. We were peeling over eighty kilograms of potatoes for my ready meal business, "Home Cooked by Hannah." To pass the time and keep our minds off the drudgery, we had created a playlist of great songs to sing to and would absolutely belt out some absolute classics (sorry, neighbours!).

It was just an ordinary day, nothing special, when a man in Spirit walked through my back door into my kitchen. He was in his early fifties, wearing a suit, with a good head of hair and a large tummy. *At least, that is what I was seeing in my mind.* "Bohemian Rhapsody" was playing and as Lorraine sang along, completely unaware of what I was experiencing, I was agog.

Was there really a man in my kitchen, smiling at me and singing along in the most beautiful baritone voice? What could this message mean? I join in and we three all sing together, although only two of us are aware of what is happening. I cannot help thinking, "Surely visitations from Spirit come when there is some sort of need or requirement? What does he want? What should I do? Is this even happening?" The song comes to an end. The classic boom of the gong sounds, and the words come into my mind, "Thanks for that ladies!" He walks back out the door. I stood there, with my mouth hanging open, for a good five minutes.

The following week at my development group, I ask for their help. Was it Spirit or have I officially lost the plot? I asked my group for their opinion and the teacher used her connection to Spirit to confirm. My group all laughed at me, it is not time for the men in white coats!

What a gift this experience was! A realisation that Spirit are *us*. They want to have fun, sing, and make us laugh. Not every interaction needs to be filled with the weight of seriousness. That they can step forward at *any* given moment and for *any* reason. I have not seen that singing man since, and I have never needed to. That small moment broke open my restricted ideas of Spirit and set me on a completely different path.

This different path has been filled with twists, turns, bumps and plunging freefalls, but I have been honoured to have learned as much as I have from Spirit. My never-ending list of questions and requests have been answered time and time again. Although it has been challenging and painful at times, I am so very grateful for my journey and the knowledge I have gained from it.

You Are a Medium (You Just Don't Know It Yet) is the book that I needed when I started my journey. I have created a guide that inspires you but also helps you to understand *why* Spirit communication works the way it does and *how* to start, improve, and maintain your connection. The answers to the questions I had that no one would answer for me.

This book is a new take on mediumship, an exploration of the unseen world beside us and the key to unlocking that power in you. If I can do it, you must certainly can!

And it will change your life.

Who am I to share this information with you?

Well… I am no one.

I am not special. I wasn't born into a family of mediums. I am not the seventh child of the seventh child or any of those things you hear about.

I was unaware of the presence of Spirit in my life until a friend connected me with my grandfather in Spirit and then everything changed.

We have all heard the stories of children awoken from their slumber by a Spirit apparition trying to communicate with them, mediums who learnt of their power when visited by a ghost unexpectedly, or oracles who have inherited this ability from a long line of seers. These stories are amazing, but they are not my experience.

I grew up fascinated by the Spirit world and mediums, but I moved through most of my life with no true awareness or personal experience with it. In, childhood, I was a confident, outspoken young person, but later became a damaged, unhappy teenager. In adulthood, I continued to be dragged by the scruff of my neck by life. I was thoughtful, sensitive, vulnerable, and so desperate for any form of love that I made some bad choices and behaved in terrible ways, both to myself and others. I felt so completely lost.

Over time I have come to learn that despite my lack of awareness, Spirit were always right there beside me! Incredibly, lack of awareness does not change Spirit's nonstop presence around us.

I do not share my history with you for sympathy; rather, I share it in hopes you find your experience relatable to mine and to so many other of us out here. The good news is you do not need to have an Earth-shattering Spiritual event in your childhood for Spirit to be there for you now.

It was at a low point in my adult life when Spirit managed to break through and contact me. I was a wife and a mother of two, cycling through the same life lessons again and again. I was completely unable to speak up for myself, suffering from a lack of self-prioritisation and zero self-love which prevented me from changing the pattern of my experience. I was being treated badly by friends and colleagues. I was being abused by myself and my own internal dialogue. And I accepted it as the way life was, telling myself to just get on with it.

I had reached a place where I just could not understand what it was all for. I had given birth to children, brought them into this world, and felt guilty about it. What legacy was I leaving them with? Here was a world corrupted by greed and uncertainty, people in power with a distinct lack of morals, society in desperate need, and others seeing this as an opportunity for self. What was the point of this? Why are we even here?

My self-esteem had reached an all-time low. I felt completely drained. I had nothing left to give, but all that life wanted to do was to take more and more from me. I was depressed and unhappy, and at the same time was berating myself and telling myself off for not being grateful for all I had.

I think we have all heard that voice at times in our life – it says something along the lines of "You have more than most people. You should be grateful. How dare you feel unhappy?" That voice is the epitome of kicking you when you are down and for the most part we say it to ourselves!

I grew close to the most amazing work colleague, Sylvia. Being around her was like being around sunshine. She was fun, upbeat, and filled with light. I knew she was a bit "woo woo" but didn't really think about it until one day she just mentioned in passing that my grandfather was communicating with her from the Spirit world.

My grandpa was the most amazing man. We had such a close bond and I loved him so much. He had been gone nearly a decade at this point, but I still missed him every day. Sylvia provided me with evidence of who he was, his personality, shared memories. But my grandfather communicated to Sylvia about things I had been doing here in the earthly realm since he had moved into Spirit. When Sylvia showed me in such an incredible, mind-blowing way that he was still around—still "alive" but in a different way—it changed the course of my life forever.

Until this point, if you had have asked me if I believed in a Spirit world I would have faltered and eventually said "yes" based more on a hope that an actual belief. But it would never have occurred to me to see a medium for a reading—and I certainly couldn't imagine that I would end up being one! Mediumship and Spirituality just was not a part of my life in any form. But what Sylvia gave me was proof—undeniable, unexplainable, concrete evidence that she was communicating with my grandfather:

- She told me my grandfather had been beside me when I had been line dancing. (I had just joined a Zumba class.)

- She told me my grandfather was aware my mother had lost her bracelet. (She had a heavy cuff bangle she had worn every day for over forty years. She had taken it off to change my daughter's nappy and left it behind on a windowsill.)

- She showed me a particular dance move he was doing. (When I was a teenager I went to my Grandparent's house for a party. Grandpa was playing his crooners music and asked me to put on a song to get the party stared. I chose "Born Slippy" just to wind him up. He called my bluff and started dancing around to it. Sylvia showed me the dance move he did in that moment.)

- She told me he had been with me when I had been skiving off work and looking for a cure for my roses. (I had been completely on my own in the office when that happened, and I had not mentioned it to her.) I asked Sylvia what cure I had discovered. When she gave me the correct answer, "vinegar," I nearly fell off my chair!

Sylvia took me to a Spiritual development circle she attended. There, I started my journey with Spirit. For those unfamiliar with a development circle, it is a gathering of people, joining in energy and intention to connect with the Spirit world. It has been traditionally called "a circle" because participants sit in a circle shape (albeit sometimes a wonky-looking circle). The energy flows around the group, connecting us heart to heart. Circles are a great space to learn as everyone gathers with the same intention. Together you can create an amazingly high frequency energy that makes Spirit connection easier, clearer, and stronger.

I went to the circle not to learn how to be a medium, but to watch the gifted workers. I could not wait to see other mediums do their thing! Maybe I would see someone else get a message like the ones I had received from Sylvia, or maybe I would be lucky enough to get another one.

Little did I realise that by attending meetings with development circle, I would be expected to take part and work! Me?! I shook my head and sat back, "I can not do this." The teacher, Jill, assured me I could.

For the first few sessions I quietly enjoyed the experience of sitting and feeling the energy, but eventually I knew it was time to try.

Although it was scary, it was the greatest gift I have ever received. Sitting in that room full of strangers and feeling the Spirit world step forward was completely life-changing. Being petrified of getting it wrong, wondering if I was making it up, and worrying that I would be judged by fellow students built a resilience in me that continues to help me every single day.

I took a deep breath and tried to tune in.

I described the energy of the Spirit guide stood beside me, a barely perceptible presence that felt like my imagination.

I felt into the guides' energy and I passed on the words of the message that popped into my head. Just random thoughts alongside all the noise in my mind, I felt like I was making it all up, surely none of this could be understood? As the recipient of the message started nodding, yes they could understand that they have been called to healing (they had just signed up for a healing course) and that their guide was presenting as an angel (they had asked the angels for the help that very morning), I just could not believe that I was right!

I was so lucky to work under the amazing tutelage of the teacher, Jill. When she asked me to vocalise what I was receiving and she validated it for me, I started understanding that <u>we can all do this</u>!

Once I started, I could not stop. I loved it. Meeting once a week with the development circle – experiencing Spirit, faith and grace was everything I had ever looked for. It was completely mind-blowing to me that I could communicate with Spirit—that they were there for me, that this ability was lying dormant within me and just needed my attention to activate it.

An amazing moment in my early days was an unexpected Spirit who stepped forward to work with – when I was not even trying to connect. This was my first ever evidential communication (where you are connecting with a loved one in the Spirit world, rather than a Spirit guide). I had been attending the development circle every week for over two years, learning to connect to, and receiving messages from, Spirit guides.

I was delivering some of my meals to a regular customer. I knew his wife had recently died and that he was really struggling, but as I knew him in a professional setting I had not even mentioned my journey with Spirit. I was unloading meals into his freezer when his wife 'walked' into the room. "Not now" I thought, as the energy in the room grew so strong it felt like the world had tipped on its axis.

"Mr. Howarth," I stuttered, "I don't want to offend you, but I have been sitting in a group to help me learn to connect to the Spirit world. I am not sure what your beliefs are, but I need to tell you your wife is here to talk to you."

"Oh, yes?" he said, not giving much away.

I then proceeded to fumble my way through some information from her; her throat felt incredibly tight, she was worried about her son, she had passed peacefully with someone holding her hand. Although Mr. Howarth nodded, he was not saying much until I mentioned a flowery bush his wife was showing me. "It has pink flowers on it," I said, "I am not good with flowers I'm afraid."

"Peony" – the word arrived in my mind so clearly, I did not doubt for a second it's validity and the declaration popped out of mouth so quickly it was almost as if Mrs. Howarth spoke it through me.

"Follow me," said Mr. Howarth, and I walked behind him as he walked down his hallway, leaning on his stick for support. I looked around in interest, I had only ever been in his kitchen, and I was nosey about the rest of his home. He took me to his living room, and there, behind some large glass sliding doors was the most beautiful pot of pink peonies.

"These were my wife's," Mr. Howarth said, "I just had the pot moved here so I can look at them from my chair and think of her."

I was gobsmacked.

Mr. Howarth then proceeded to tell me about his wife. She was a Spiritualist Reiki Master so they both knew all about mediumship and how it works. Their son has been struggling at work, she had passed from throat cancer and her passing had been peaceful, Mr. Howarth was there, holding her hand. I was awed by the cleverness of the Spirit world, knowing that it would be safe for me to communicate with her as he understood Spirit, and taking me by surprise so I could not get in my own way.

I left Mr. Howarth a bit watery eyed and sat in my car, shaking. Did that really just happen? What was that? Could I do it again if I wanted to?

The connection to Mrs. Howarth was mind blowing but also unique. To this day, it is one of only a handful of times that Spirit have approached me to pass on a message. The majority of mediumship is you opening up with intention to communicate, and that is a very different experience. As soon as you are seeking information you create an energy around you that makes it harder and less natural. This book gives you the information you need to overcome that resistant energy, understanding how Spirit communication works and the process you need to go through to make it happen!

Fast forward a decade since Mr. & Mrs. Howarth and a LOT of development, hard work and determination and I am a professional evidential medium and Spiritual teacher. I have a top-ten Spiritual development podcast and yet I am still on a journey of development. I feel I have barely scratched the surface of all there is to know.

But there is so much more than the label of my job – I am happy... truly happy. In fact, I am life-affirmingly joyous (perhaps sometimes nauseatingly so). I laugh often, and I mean <u>really</u> laugh. I make choices based on what will bring me the most happiness, not on the clinical list of demands my brain naturally provides.

I know, I know. You are probably rolling your eyes right now. If I had read the previous paragraph in 2005 I would have been gagging all over place. And yet, here we are.

That is my inspiration for this book. Connection to Spirit has completely changed the way I experience my life. I want this for you, too. I am so fed up with the rhetoric from mediums that they have a gift, and that you don't. Spirit communication is a natural process for all of us, and opening up to that world is transformational and life affirming.

You want to be happier? Feel loved? Achieve more? Choose joy and contentment over pain and stress? Reconnect with loved ones who have passed over?

Spirit can help inspire and ignite you. Spirit can love you until you love yourself better (and after that, too). Spirit can prove their existence to even the most analytical, doubting minds (they've had to work incredibly hard for me).

And they are with you, right now.

Let's get started

I'm asking you for a little bit of commitment here. It requires a willing suspension of disbelief (in your own abilities). It involves an open mindset of "what if?". It necessitates allowing yourself to hope. It insists that you release that armour of protection and safety that is born of cynicism. It obligates you to endure the vulnerability of your own potential. It may sound like that's asking a lot, but you can do this. The only thing stopping you is yourself. You already bought this book; what do you have to lose?

Just keep reading. Keep going.

This is just the beginning for you. You should not settle and accept that you will do mediumship exactly the way that I do it. Use this book as a foundation. Regard it as the seeds that will eventually grow into your own unique style of mediumship, your individual relationship with the Spirit world. Your relationship with Spirit and your mediumship is yours and yours alone.

How to use this book

This book is the culmination of years of development, study, practice and guidance from my Spirit team, the product of my inquisitive mind who could never just settle for how it has always been done. I asked Spirit to help me learn and they delivered. Not every lesson has been comfortable, but every lesson has been worthwhile.

Over the next twelve chapters we will dive into the mechanics of mediumship, the different ways of receiving energy and how to work with this power to unfold your own gifts.

We are going to start with the Foundations – the basis for all Spiritual communication and development, if you do not hold the information in this chapter you are going to find it a *lot* harder to connect than it should be. In chapter 3 we discover the Spirit world itself – where are these beings you are trying to connect to? In chapter 4 we explore your own energy body and how your vibration impacts your mediumistic abilities, followed by a chapter dedicated to doubt – something we all must face and work through on this journey. Then we look at Spooky Stuff – the high-profile version of the Spirit world seen in films and stories, but is any of that a true reflection of Spirit? Chapter 7 is delving into the process – how does mediumship work? Over the following chapters we will expand into the Five Frequencies of Spirit work: Psychic, Healing, Spirit Guides, Evidential and Trance. Before ending with a chapter with activities to deepen your connection and give you opportunities for practice.

I have laid out these chapters in the way that I teach. After years of teaching students and helping them to explore their own abilities, I have learnt the easiest way for most people to unfold their mediumship. I believe you need to understand the how and why so you can then move into this work with a comfortable foundation, knowledge really is power.

I want to start your journey by telling you this one, very important, thing.

I believe in you.

I really do. On your mediumship development journey you will doubt yourself, second guess your evidence and have to face your own self again and again and again. That is the journey, and there is no easy way around this. Many fall off this path, purely because they let their own self doubt stop them. I am the working example of what can happen if you push through that resistance. I still face my own fear *every single time* I work. But I won't let it beat me. I love mediumship too much for that.

It is normal to feel afraid. It is normal to doubt. It is normal to think you are making it up.

I believe in you.

Just try. Just take the step. Make the jump. Ignore the doubt for the next few minutes.

Until you start to feel Spirit's belief in you.

And when you start to feel that, really *feel* it. Pull it in to you. Absorb it into every molecule of your being. Breathe it in. Allow it.

Until one day, you will realise… you believe in you, too.

2
Foundations

Before we go too far, let me explain some of the terminology in this book. One of the interesting things in Spiritual development I have found so far, is that different mediums and teachers use different words to explain the same thing. It is confusing! So here is my take and how I will be using the words in this book:

Spirit – any person or animal in the Spirit world. Some will have lived physical lives here on Earth and some will not have.

Spirit World – the place where the Spirits are. I used to view it as heaven; a place far away from here where we go when we die. I have changed my mind about this, more about this later!

Medium – a person who is an interpreter of energies. Like a translator, they speak both their human language and the language of energy, which can take the form of words, pictures, feelings and more! Mediums can work with Spirit and also with people still here in the physical world to share the information and guidance they are receiving.

Mediumship – the act of tuning into energy and translating it into words.

Sitter – a person who is receiving a message or healing from Spirit, via a medium.

What follows is my Truths of Spirit communication. In my experience, these are immovable, things I have found to always be true when working with Spirit. It has really helped my development and understanding to have these in place, to know that however I am receiving and experiencing the lessons, guidance & information from Spirit these rules remain constant and true.

THE TRUTHS OF SPIRIT COMMUNICATION

1) **There are NO rules!**
   Your relationship with Spirit is yours alone. The more natural and organic that relationship is, the more profound and life changing it is. This book is designed as a guide to start you off, to open the door. Once you are through that door, the most important part of your development is to then discover how your relationship with Spirit works for <u>you</u>. Be open, be willing to start from scratch many times, let your team inspire you, and light your own way.

2) **Spirits are ALWAYS with you**
   They are not off somewhere else; they do not take breaks. Heaven really is a place on Earth. I always imagined myself calling them in from another dimension–disturbing their heavenly peaceful experience–but they were right beside me all that time. The Spirit world is not somewhere we go after death, it is somewhere we already are! Our world is contained within the Spirit world; there is no separation.

3) **Spirit are unlimited power and energy**
   Unlimited means exactly that. You are not bothering them. You are not taking energy that could be meant for someone else. There is an abundance for all. More than that, Spirit LOVE to be asked to work with you. This connection brings them nothing but joy. They experience what we experience. Do not hold back; invite them in!

4) **Spirit are a force for good only**
   Spirit are playful, knowledgeable and positive. They never judge, berate, or scare you. They only want for you to be happy and open up to your fullest potential. If you experience anything else, it is your preconceptions holding your experience back. This will be gently resolved within your practice (if you remain open to this) as you unfold and remember what your soul already knows.

5) **Spirit bring unconditional love**
   Spirit's love is completely unconditional. It has no limits. It is given to you as you are right now... perfectly imperfect. They do not want you to change, unless that change will make you happier. They do not care about your past, your dress size, or if your teeth need brushing; they love you as you are! They do not expect you to be anything other than a human—questioning, doubting, judging, and getting it wrong sometimes. We are here for a human experience and all that it entails. We are not here to be a Spirit. If our soul wanted that, we could have remained in the nonphysical realm!

6) **Spirit need your trust**
   Information received from Spirit might not always make sense to you, but from our limited human perception, very little does! We have to learn to take the steps that seem illogical, give the evidence that seems nonsensical, and follow the path that appears to lead away from what we have asked for. Spirit <u>always</u> come through. Their guidance always ultimately makes sense. They always know the best route to send us for that ultimate outcome. It is <u>us</u> that gets in the way!

7) **Spirit obey your free will and choice**
   The universe runs on this law. You choose and they give you what you ask for. If you say, "no," they stop immediately. If you choose to ignore your intuition and make choices that are not right for you, they will let you. You are the one in charge. And, yes, this means that the only thing holding you back is yourself!

The Valve Theory

Let me introduce you to one of the most beneficial things Spirit have taught me in my development; The Valve Theory. I wanted to know why sometimes I could get a great connection to energy, and sometimes it seemed impossible to me. And why is it that sometimes it feels like Spirit have moved further away from me, rather than coming closer?

This is all down to <u>my</u> energy, rather than how the Spirit or sitter is communicating with me. And it is the same for you. Spirit showed me my energy as covered in hundred upon thousands of tiny valves. These valves have the ability to open you up to the energy you are working with, but they can also close and cut you off.

Visualize your aura (the energy body that surrounds you). Imagine it looking like a giant, egg-shaped invisible balloon. Take a couple of deep breaths and allow yourself to really hold that visualisation.

Now imagine the boundary of your aura covered in hundreds upon thousands of tiny valves. To me, these valves look like a piece of copper plumbing, with a simple on/off mechanism. You might imagine these differently, and that is absolutely fine. Go with what works for you.

To communicate with Spirit, some of these valves need to be open. The more valves that are open, the stronger and clearer your connection will be.

Some of these valves will open up naturally as you work on prioritising yourself and raising your vibration.

Some of these valves will be closed down by your own self-doubt and negative expectations.

Some of these valves will be opened by experience, the more you work with Spirit the more naturally open your valves are – practice, practice and practice some more!

Some of these valves will be closed by stress and low vibration emotions.

Some of these valves will be opened by your conscious intention.

The good news is that none of these valves are sealed permanently. However, you will need to practice to try to open up as many as you can. That is how I can connect easily to Spirit. I just have more valves open. Simple.

A lack of belief in your own abilities keeps your valves closed. Let me say that again, because it is so important:

A lack of belief in your own abilities prevents you from receiving information from the Spirit world.

It does not mean that they aren't there. It means that when you do not believe in yourself, you close yourself off from them. You close your valves and then wonder why you cannot feel them beside you.

Always try to remember; if you feel that Spirit have stepped back or are not even stepping forward to work with you, <u>they have not gone anywhere</u>. They are still right there, beside you. You are not being punished for not being good enough. I hear students say to me often "they've gone" – Spirit have never gone. They would never leave you hanging. They want to work with you as much as you want to work with them.

When this happens to me, as it still does, I take some deep breaths and I remember. I remember what I know; that Spirit *love* me. That the only true failing is to give up. I imagine some of my valves gently opening and I visualise a golden, glittery light from Spirit running through them. I breathe into that love from Spirit and I allow myself to relax.

When I start any form of mediumship work affirm myself into my valves opening:

- "I am a phenomenal medium. I get evidence with ease & clarity.
- I am a phenomenal medium. I get evidence with ease & clarity.
- I am a phenomenal medium. I get evidence with ease & clarity."

You can use any affirmation you like. I have worked with several over the years, although this has been mine since I started stepping out onto a stage to demonstrate mediumship.

As a suggestion, if you find the one above too much, you can start with:

"Spirit are with me. I am loved. I can do this".

Say this in your head, or out loud three times (as a minimum, I say affirmations to myself all day every day when I am working, and three times just before I go on stage).

You have got this! I believe in you.

3
The Spirit World

You are *already* living in the Spirit world!

Most people think of the Spirit world as a separate place – a place we go after we die. It is perfectly reasonable and logical to believe the Spirit world is separate because we are most aware and connected with our *physical* experience on this planet. In comparison, the Spirit world is generally *nonphysical* and therefore less apparent. It is therefore natural for our human minds, in our physical body, to imagine a separate place where the nonvisible, nonphysical exists.

However, I want you to think of the Spirit world and physical world co-existing as a single place. Rather than being separate, think of our physical experience as a different dimension of the same space. I imagine it as if we are a physical world contained and immersed in the Spirit world. That is right – we are *already* in the Spirit world. There is no separation. There is no going "somewhere else." We are in a physical form for a period (our "lifetime") and we leave that form when our physical bodies cease to live. But even while we are in physical form, a part of us is nonphysical. You can call it a "soul," a "consciousness," or an "energy," – there are many names for it – but that aspect of us is inseparable from the Spirit world. It always has been part of the Spirit world and will be for eternity.

We have all chosen to come here to Earth for the experience. With that choice, part of your consciousness became embodied in the physical body you find yourself in right now. You are a human, but you are also a Spirit.

Spirit gave me an analogy by showing me an image in my mind's eye of wearing a virtual reality headset. While wearing the headset, you are completely immersed in that space. You are not fully aware of the physical world around you, unless someone talks to you, or you accidentally walk into the furniture! The concept is the same with the Spirit world. Our souls are wearing a virtual reality headset that creates a physical existence for us. We can be aware of aspects of the nonphysical realm, but we are unable to fully comprehend it until we remove the headset, leaving our physical selves behind.

A limitation of existing in the physical realm is we are naturally less aware of the Spirit world. This condition serves an important purpose, because if you were still experiencing the Spirit world in the same way that your soul does, you would find it impossible to live a normal human life. In that case, there would be no point in coming here!

Your soul, that consciousness within you, communicates with you nonstop. However, we are not listening that often! We are conditioned from birth to use and rely on our external senses for information and validation. As you grow, society's training discourages those abilities that are more closely connected to communicating with spirit. This is why children can often experience Spirit more easily than adults.

Your soul is trying to communicate – *listen!*

Despite all this, you have heard your own soul trying to communicate with you, haven't you? There was that time you wanted to turn down an invitation to a party, but you ignored your instincts and went, only to bump into your ex and his new girlfriend. There was also that one time you said "Yes," but you knew in your heart you should be saying "No," and when it all went wrong you thought "I knew I should have said, 'No.'" You had that experience when you had a feeling something was happening at home and dialled the number only to have your partner answer with "Thank goodness you called! I need you." You have that sense that someone you know is not okay no matter what they are saying or that smile they are painting on their face.

Everyone has a list of these examples. Everyone receives messages from their intuition. Everyone has a gut instinct. But often we just choose not to listen. Our human condition leads us to be mentally overloaded. We are stimulated to the point of chaos. We are disempowered by the constant needs of the world around us, and our own happiness is given less importance.

Your soul is striving to be heard over that noise. Just because you cannot always hear it doesn't mean it is not talking to you. It is always communicating. Your soul is telling you what is right for you – it is your emotional instinct, the feeling that rises from within you. It is not tangible. It may not make sense to you intellectually, but it is still a communication.

When I look back, most examples of my inner knowing working fell in the category of "I knew I shouldn't have done that!" *after* the event, rather than "Thank goodness I listened" *before* it happened. It is so hard to trust that voice. It is hard to pay attention to the quietest, softest experience in a world with such loud and harsh noise. I would like to tell you that I never miss a message from myself any longer, but sometimes my human side still manages to get in the way! The problem is, for most of us, our brain overrides the voice of our soul.

My perfect example of this is a time when I joined a yoga class. I spoke to the teacher about joining and I was so excited. She warned me "I need you here ten minutes before the class starts to complete the forms and have a chat." On the day of the first class, I arrived super early at the hall where the yoga class was to be held. At that time, I was still running around like a crazy person, not at all in control of my experience. I was learning in my development group, confident in my connection with my guides, but I was still challenging their guidance, ignoring advice for myself whilst choosing to dole it out to others like a patronising pseudo-Buddha.

I reverse parked easily into the perfect spot and wound my window down to sit with my face in the sun. It was bliss. I made the mistake of looking at my phone and saw that message had come through from a friend. They lived down the road from the class, but they had woken up late and were asking for a lift. My instinct said, "Do not do it." But my brain said, "You are a bad friend! You have got loads of time. Go and pick her up. Don't be selfish. What is wrong with you?"

I went to pick her up. On the way I got stuck in a queue of cars behind a rubbish truck. It was taking forever! I finally got to her house. The clock was ticking. She was not ready. I waited outside, getting stressed. She finally came out. I was snappy and grumpy with her because I was now supposed to be at the class completing my forms. We went down the road, and the rubbish truck was still there. I turned around, trying an alternative route. Of course, that road was blocked by a lorry delivering furniture! Did a 36-point turn to go back the original way and got stuck behind the rubbish truck again.

When I finally arrived at the hall, there were no parking spaces. I managed to make the class with only seconds to spare. I received a telling-off from the teacher for holding everyone up to complete my forms because I was late.

I sat on my mat, feeling stressed, embarrassed, and fed up. This was not the relaxing, connecting experience I was hoping for. I did not understand how it worked with Spirit at that point and I felt cheated. When I asked Spirit why they had let that happen, I (quite rightly) got short shrift: "We told you not to go. You felt that instinct to say no to that message. You ignored it. You ignored us." Here is part of the problem – when it comes to communicating with Spirit, we often ignore our humble emotions and expect something bigger, stronger, and more definitive. I wish I could tell you that I learned my lesson, but I really had not! Our human condition easily leads us to ignore the message and information we receive on a daily basis. I try hard to listen, but I am not perfect, nor will I ever be.

Do you feel that emotion? It is Spirit communication. Do you hear your instinct calling? It is Spirit communication. Do you sense that thought bubbling up amongst the noise, asking you to listen? It is Spirit communication. We are communicating with Spirit all the time, but Spirit is not separate from us. Understanding and developing this connection is the foundation of all mediumship. You communicate with other Spirits through your own Spirit. If you are not listening to, and honouring your own Spirit, you cannot expect to communicate with the rest of the Spirit world.

Activity 1: Listening In

This activity asks you to tune into your *self*. In order to be able to feel the subtlety of Spirit, to experience the quietest and gentlest of energies you will firstly need to know what your own energy is saying. To know what is Spirit and what is you, you need to know what *you* feel like. Spirit communication is experienced through your energetic, emotional and sometimes physical body. To be aware of what your human self is bringing up within you is instrumental in being aware of what is being shown to you by the Spirit world. It is also a great chance to start the process of putting words to feeling, much of mediumship is finding the language to describe something that you are energetically experiencing. It is challenging enough to do this in your own space, let alone to do in when altering your perception to communicate with Spirit.

Sit in a quiet space where you will not be disturbed. Have some paper and a pen with you. Maybe now is a good time to treat yourself to a beautiful new notebook and a pen you like writing with? Although not at all necessary, the ceremony of opening that fresh book feels like a new start, the beginning of your journey, writing with a lovely pen make this moment special and sacred. But even if you're writing on the back of your gas bill it will still work!

Set yourself a timer. I suggest 5 minutes to begin with.

Write down any thoughts that are coming to mind. What is your brain saying? If your mind is like mine, it will instantly start to produce a list of things you need to do or things you may have forgotten. That is okay. Write them down. Now that you have moved that list out of your mind and onto your paper, you should not worry about forgetting them. What else is on your mind?

You may find yourself wondering how much is left on the timer. You may be itching to pick up your phone or work on crossing that high priority, time-sensitive item off your "to do" list. Can you just sit with yourself? Can you hold a space for you? Be determined. What else is coming up for you?

Follow your breath, the gentle in and out. Feel the rise and fall of your chest.

This is not meditating. This is just *being*. Do not shut your eyes and escape to another space. Be present with yourself. Be peaceful. Be still.

If imagery is helpful for you, imagine your energy looking like a giant snow globe. Life has a way of shaking it all up, doesn't it? Watch the swirling energy gradually slow down and flutter gently, as it settles to the bottom.

When you feel calm, settled, and still, ask yourself these three questions and write down the answers:

1) How does my body feel?
2) What are my emotions telling me?
3) If I was tuning in to my soul, what would it say?

You can repeat this activity as often as you like. I recommend focusing on settling your energy several times a day. The more adept you become at settling and being fully present with yourself, the easier you will find it to communicate with Spirit.

4
Vibration Rising

When mediums talk about communicating with Spirit, you often hear words such as "frequency," "vibration" and "power" mentioned, without real context, so I thought I would start this chapter with what I mean when I am using these terms.

Frequency: This is you choosing which band of energy you are working in. I teach the Five Frequencies approach to mediumship. These frequencies are available to us to receive and interpret energy: Psychic, Spirit Guide, Evidential, Healing & Trance. To choose your frequency is as simple as having the thought "I am working with my Spirit guides now" to "I want to work psychically now". I visualise a light switch with a small label under each switch. I turn on the one I want to work in. Of course, Spirit are an intelligence way beyond our understanding, but we live in a Universe of free will and choice. This means we choose what we do with our energy and intention, they cannot do it for us. Often, developing mediums believe that Spirit choose which frequency we are in – they do not. We choose it, and we can move through those frequencies instantly. We delve into the Five Frequencies later in this book, but for now it is enough to know you receive what you have tuned in to. You only want to tune into one frequency at a time, in order to have the strongest and clearest connection in that space.

Vibration: Imagine the energy of a human being, think of it on a usual daily basis as a moving scale between zero and one hundred. Constantly changing, shifting and moving, your rating on this scale changes minute by minute. The lower end of the scale is for people that think negatively, see the glass half empty and decide to focus on what is wrong, rather than seeking out what is right. Similarly, the top of the scale is for people who have reprogrammed their thoughts, choose joy and gratitude over resentment and worry. By default, humans are at a lower frequency that the Spirit world as we have incarnated into a physical, denser, lower vibrational body. Now imagine Spirit, if we are at a maximum of one hundred, they are easily at level one hundred *thousand*, if not more! The Spirit world is the highest vibration in the universe. When communicating with Spirit your job is to shift your vibration into an altered state, moving beyond the maximum one hundred rating on the scale. Spirit will meet you where you are, but the higher your vibrational rate, the easier and clearer you will find Spirit communication. The greatest gift you can give yourself in your Spiritual unfoldment is to work on your mindset, assist your energy with healing and make sure you are nurturing yourself – this means you will be at a higher vibration before you start to open up to Spirit. Within the lower, physical band of energy there are many different frequencies we can sit in. Frequencies can change easily and quickly and are completely dependent on our emotions and where our attention goes. Our vibrational rate can, and does, change instantly and often!

Power: Power is the energy that is built from you as the medium, alongside your helpers in the Spirit world. When I am getting ready to work with Spirit I take three deep, long, breaths. As I do this I imagine my energy expanding and radiating out of me, getting bigger and brighter and stronger. It does not take long as I have been practising this for some time, and I now trust that it will happen instantly. Then once I start working with the Spirit, I find my power continues to expand and grow. If you are new to Spiritual development, I suggest you work on your healing (see forthcoming chapter on healing) first, followed by a daily intentional practice of breathing into your energy, expanding your power, holding it for a few minutes and then letting that energy dissipate. Once you start working with Spirit on a regular basis this will happen naturally and without any concerted effort.

I think it is important at this stage to remind you that when your soul chose to come here to live an earthly experience, only a small part of that magnificent, multifaceted being that is you moved into this realm. The rest of you remains in the Spirit world, often referred to as your Higher Self. So even though you are here in the physical world, you are also in the Spirit world right now, too. You are Spirit.

When I interviewed Emily and her Stars on my podcast, she used a great analogy to explain this; your soul is like an orange – the part that is here in your physical body is one segment. The whole orange is your entire soul. It is part of you here, experiencing the physical, but the greater part of you remains in the Spirit world.

The higher your vibration, the easier and more natural communication with your Higher Self becomes. It is not like communicating with a separate being at all, just an amazing, all knowing all seeing supportive energy of love that guides and inspires you through your thoughts, feelings and instincts. I believe that all Spirit communication is through your Higher Self – through a clear and easy channel to that being is the access to all beings.

The fragment of your soul that incarnated here is high vibration, but impacted by your physical self, including your thoughts and feelings. The frequency we sit at has a direct correlation with our experience here on Earth. If we are sitting in a lower vibration we attract lower vibrational experiences. If we are sitting in a higher vibration we attract more of the good stuff!

Your Role in Changing Frequencies

Most students I have worked with believe that connecting to Spirit is an external process – that they will leave themselves and float off into the ether with a choir of angels and a rainbow cloud. They hope that the journey with Spirit will take them away from themselves, the parts of them they do not like, their life they are dissatisfied with – that Spirit will help them to escape.

Communicating with Spirit will help you to heal, change your life, and feel better. However, I believe we need to start this process in reverse. If you want to communicate with Spirit, you need to make your frequency compatible with Spirit.

Think of yourself like an old-fashioned ariel television – the channel you are tuned into is the one that you play. The frequency of your energy defines your physical experience. Which station are you receiving right now? Are you on the channel with the show you have watched too many times – the one where everything seems to go wrong all at once? Is the one that starts the day getting out the "wrong side of the bed" and then the whole day is filled with mishaps? If so, you are on the wrong channel!

Tuning into a positive station changes your life. I know, I know… that sounds a bit "airy fairy," but it works!

Once you find yourself on a better channel, you will have to work at staying on it. You will have to ensure you do not allow other people's lower frequencies to interfere with yours. When you hit the inevitable bumps on the road of life, you must try not let those circumstances stop you from holding onto the higher vibration of where you want to be!

When I first worked with Spirit, I thought they would help me to change my life – to rid myself of those things that were holding me back. I thought that Spirit would help me to rise. And they did! However, they did it by making *me* accountable for it, by pushing back at all my excuses and all my barriers.

The journey of clear Spirit communication starts with making sure your energy is at the highest vibrational frequency it can be. Yes, Spirit are always with you, but in your human form, it is easier to experience Spirit from a higher frequency.

When you are having a difficult time, it can feel like Spirit has deserted you. Of course, Spirit have not gone anywhere. They do not punish us for our experiences and choices. Spirit are a source of *truly unconditional* love. But when we are weighed down by our experiences and emotions, it is simply harder to feel Spirit.

Vibrational Frequency and Healing

We expect the Spiritual journey to be a journey *out*, but it is actually a journey *in*. Much of your Spiritual development journey will be focused on healing, and I am not just referring to Spiritual healing. Part of your work will be to discover what it is your physical, mental, and emotional needs. I am a great believer in therapy, exercise, and medication. (Treading the line between mass pharma and what you need to be able to live a healthy happy life, I am aware of the dangers in the world we face, but I also know I would not be writing this book without my hormone medication that has changed my life). We discuss healing in more depth later in this chapter.

Once you are communicating with Spirit, your understanding of self will grow. This will, in turn, help your healing further. To me, the interdependent cycle of Spirit communication and healing looks like this:

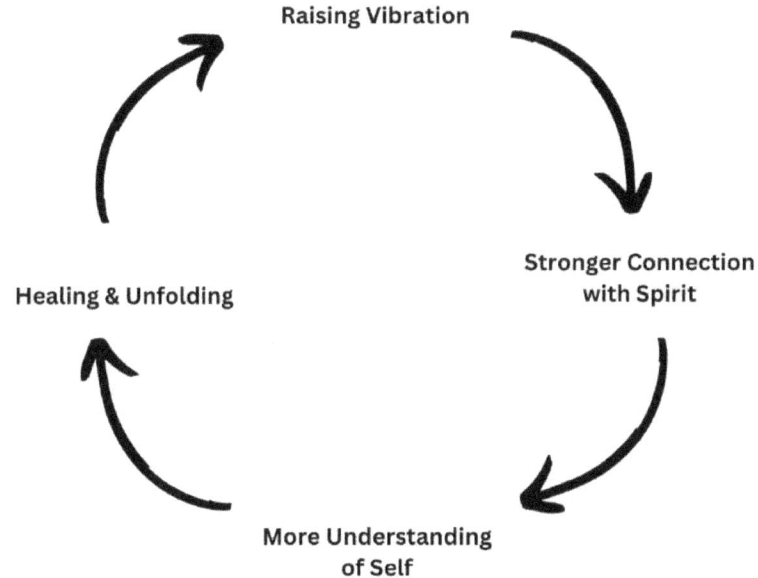

It is important to understand that Spirit will not ever override your free will and choice. This is one of the laws of the universe. If you make choices that are not compatible with your energy, if you ignore or forget to listen to your instincts, your vibration will suffer as a result. *You* are in charge of your channel!

The Energy Diet

Every individual is impacted by what I call their "energy diet." This is exactly what it sounds like! Rather than counting calories, looking at just the food you are consuming, etc., I want you to look at what you are allowing into your energy and the impact (both negative and positive) this has on you. And just like food diets, different things can affect each of us differently! I would love to give you an easy formula for your diet, but I cannot. We are all different. Only *you* can discover your diet plan for yourself. It starts with paying attention.

For example, I cannot watch the news. The stories of sadness and hurt deeply affect my vibration. The flip side of this is most of the time I have no idea what's going on. It drives my husband mad! In comparison, I have Spiritually-connected friends who watch the news with no problem, but are significantly impacted by caffeine!

The most important thing you can do is work out what is impacting you, and then manage it. Put simply: Consume more of what makes you feel good and less of what does not!

As your energy evolves, you will find yourself stronger and less impacted by certain circumstances, while other experiences that you can bear easily now will become harder for you in time. It can also change day to day, hour to hour, minute to minute. This is perfectly normal. Energy is always moving, changing, and shifting.

You can further strengthen and increase your frequency by being thankful. Live that "attitude of gratitude," by actively seeking out positives in your days and making sure you take time to do things that bring you joy. No matter how small or fleeting these things are, you will create bigger and more vibrant experiences by revelling in the ones you are currently experiencing.

Being mindful of your energy diet is not about avoiding things that need to be dealt with. If, for example, you are being negatively impacted by your mental health, you may need to seek professional help to deal with this. I see too many Spiritual people preaching "Spiritual bypassing". This is not about avoiding what is rising within you or burying trauma under a veil of positivity and pretending everything is ok. This is about making choices that support your happiness and wellness. If you need to eat better and exercise, no amount of Spirit connection will take that physical need away. But, you may find you have more energy to give yourself when you stop haemorrhaging it on things you cannot help or have no control over. If you need therapy, go get therapy. If you need exercise, take a walk. If you need to drink more water, for goodness' sake, go and get yourself a glass now!

I want to be clear that there are some experiences that you will not be able to heal from. Just surviving them and rebuilding your life is enough. I am not talking about those experiences when I am talking about healing. Deep trauma, grief and loss does not go away. You will walk with those wounds for the rest of your life. You will grow around these experiences and tread a different path. But they cannot be wiped out and erased.

Unfortunately, we do not experience a life here where everything is rosy. You will experience difficult times, frustrations, and people being very... well... human! The key here is to try and let the negatives pass you by. Do not focus on them. Do what needs to be done and move on. Limit the amount of attention you give them. Also, milk the positives for every single little drop of energy they have. Focus on them. Replay them. Celebrate them. Daydream on them.

Remember that energy is constantly fluctuating, expanding, and shifting. What impacts your energy today may not be the same next week, and it certainly will not be the same next year. Always pay attention to what works for you and what does not. Allow yourself to shift and change with these fluctuations. One of the hardest things to overcome is the human desire for things to be set in stone – when it comes to Spirit and your development, nothing is.

Activity 2: Day Review

Make sure you take 10 minutes every day (preferably at the end of the day) to think about your experiences throughout the day and remember how you felt! What felt good? What felt like it was pulling you down? Being aware of this is the first step. What can you learn from the negatives? What were you teaching you? Why did you experience that?

Now, focus your thoughts onto the good parts of your day and sit for a short while enjoying the memories of the good stuff and being grateful for it. Give thanks to the universe for these experiences. If something negative creeps in, that is okay. Just acknowledge it and move past it back onto the happy things. If you have had a bad day, week, or month, do not worry! We all have them. They are part of the human experience. Just cast your mind back to a memory that brings you joy.

Do this every day for a month. See how this starts to change your mindset, and see how that starts to clear the path for connection.

Activity 3: Attitude of Gratitude

Every hour of the waking day, find something to be grateful for, and send a little thought of thanks to it. It does not have to be massive stuff, and it does not have to be stuff you have got yet!

For example, you will often catch me saying, "thank you" for:

- The birds on my feeder,
- The wind for blowing through my energy,
- Coffee being the best and most delicious thing in the world,
- The holiday we are going to have next year and have not even booked yet, or
- My shoes for being so damn comfy!

And this list doesn't include all the wonderful people in my life who bring me such happiness. (Just FYI, I don't say my "thank you's" out loud. I'm not asking you to invite funny looks from your colleagues. Just saying it in your head is fine!)

Your energy is a garden. Feed the flowers not the weeds!

The frequency of what you focus on brings more of that frequency into your life. It is like a cartoon of a snowball rolling down a mountain. It starts small, but before you know it, the snowball has become the size of a house – and taking you with it!

I am aware that both of these activities seem a bit cutesy. When I was in such desperate need at the beginning of my journey and Spirit suggested this approach to me, I thought it was a pile of... well... crap. But part of me knew I needed to do it. Even though my brain sneered at it, I did it, <u>and this changed my life</u>.

I am not saying I do not have bad days. I am not saying I float through life on a soft candy pink cloud, unmoved from my state of bliss and joy by the humdrum of existence. I am saying that these simple activities started a chain reaction in me. They helped me to understand how much my mindset contributed to my experience. I realized my limiting beliefs that there was not enough, and that I was in competition with others, prevented me from growing the way that I could have. Yes, these things are small, but if you take many small things, they soon add up to something much bigger.

One of the biggest hurdles to overcome on a healing journey is self-prioritisation. This is something you are going to have to get comfortable with if you want to work with Spirit. Sometimes life will not align for you. It will not be easy. It will not be straightforward. During those times, you will need to prioritise your desire to heal, change, and work with Spirit over other aspects and people in your life.

This is a speech I make in every beginner's course I teach. We all have this idea that Spirit will make it happen for us, that they will clear a path. Sometimes, they do not. Although it can be frustrating, it is important for our development. Sometimes the learning we need comes from prioritising our journey with the Spirit world instead of expecting them to do it for us. Do not buy into the idea that if it is meant for you, it will be easy for you. This is the most disempowering suggestion I have ever heard!

Get comfortable with the idea that <u>if you want it, you are going to have to show up for it</u>. Some days will be easier than others. We expect so much from Spirit. From the moment we connect, we start asking and demanding and wanting. And that is fine. It is expected. It is enjoyed and celebrated!... As long as when it does not happen how you expected, you don't feel cheated. There were times in my journey when I thought Spirit had not made it easy as some form of divine punishment, but now I can also see the growth from these moments.

Sometimes you have to prioritise what you want. And sometimes it is completely necessary to get where you need to be. Are you waiting for everyone else to be sorted before you take a step for you? Are you asking Spirit to clear your decks so you can focus on them? Are you playing yourself one of these stories?

- Once X is done, then I will do it.
- Once X is okay, then I will focus on what I want.
- X needs me, but once they are sorted, I'll focus on me.

What if the biggest lesson you need right now is that Spirit are with you, that they have always been with you, and that you need to choose yourself in order to connect to them? More than that, if working with Spirit comes from a deep connection with our true self, how are you going to grow that connection and get it to where it needs to be if you spend all your time ignoring your needs and only focusing on others?

We think that the Spirit world will take us from Point A to Point B because we have asked them to. They will, but the Spirit world know (in their infinite wisdom) that to get us to Point B, we need to first experience Points A.1, A.2, and A.3. Sometimes in this journey, it can feel like things are not happening the way that we want, but we are actually going in exactly the direction we need to.

When I decided I wanted to start offering readings to the public and working as a professional medium, the Spirit world was delighted! They had been encouraging me along this path for some time, but that did not mean that I didn't need refinement. They sent me clients and lessons that I needed to develop my offering, strengthen my resilience, and empower my business. For example:

- The client who did not turn up, and when I called to see where they were said "I thought you were psychic. Shouldn't you have known I was not coming?" taught me to charge upfront at booking.
- The students who told me they knew better than me, and to whom I gave my power, taught me boundaries and determination.
- The colleagues who took advantage of my good nature from their own space of greed and lack, and who tried to steal clients from me, taught me that I need to have trust in myself, that I am as important in my readings as my work is, and they could not steal the essence of my business, because they are not me!
- The client who was not interested and did the washing up while I was reading for them taught me to stop offering gift vouchers. (They were not invested in having a reading so they were not committed to the experience.)
- The countless trolls and keyboard warriors who taught me to be strong and have great boundaries, and also that not everyone is ready to hear about Spirit.

- The non-believers who made me question my own faith and go deeper with my understanding. (I recognise more about the growth in respectful discussion and the times when I need to value my own energy and attention.)

There are so many examples like this. At the time, they will hurt, but once you can move past your emotional response, you will understand the purpose these experiences serve. Spirit know the best way to get you from where you are to where you want to be. It is up to us to trust the journey.

Recently, I did a demonstration in a town that was new to me. As I was driving through the town centre, it was rush hour. Cars were cutting in from every angle, there were countless traffic lights, crowded roundabouts, and beeping horns. Two cars in front of me, I saw a poor woman whose car had been smashed into by a van. The van's driver had pulled up alongside her car and left his vehicle blocking the road. I had to force myself out onto the wrong side of the road and into incoming traffic to be able to get past. It was not a comfortable space for me as a driver! It really reminded me though of my mindset at the beginning of my Spiritual journey. A complicated moment like this would have made me think Spirit did not want me to demonstrate at that venue, that maybe it was a warning, or an omen. Luckily, I have moved beyond that kind of mindset now. I know that if I want it and I create it, Spirit will make it happen for me. I made it to the venue. It was blummin' fantastic and I can honestly say it was my best work so far!

Activity 4: Prioritising Yourself

Do something for yourself *everyday* – whether it is having a cup of tea in your favourite mug, gathering a bunch of daffodils, having a good soak in the bath, indulging in an episode of *The Witcher*, savouring a bar of chocolate, or sipping a glass of nice wine. Honour yourself, every day, no excuses.

Guess what? It is harder in practice than you think it is going to be! Start with 15 minutes as a target. You may find it tough but be determined. Do not let your programming get the better of you. This shows you the commitment you need to make. You must commit to yourself to commit to Spirit. If you miss a day or two, that fine. Just keep going when you can. Fight with yourself to make you the focus for a while. Try to do this every day.

This activity is not supposed to make you feel guilty or for you to berate yourself for getting it wrong sometimes. It is designed to draw your attention to the things that need changing, to how much (or how little) of your day is focused on you and your needs. Spirit cannot do this bit for you. Remembering the rule of free will and choice, this activity is designed so that you realise how little you choose you, and how hard it is to rectify that.

It does get easier! We are aiming for you to start to do this naturally, without effort. But it will take time to change your mental patterns and for others in your life to understand the "new" you. Be patient with yourself as you explore this new outlook, but firm as you take just 15 minutes a day for you.

The Staircase

Imagine your frequency as a flight of stairs. As you start to prioritise yourself, to take time for you, to watch your energy diet, and make choices accordingly, you take steps up the stairs. Your physical self at the lowest point is right down at the bottom of the stairs. Your nonphysical soul self is at the top – way off in the distance, too far away to see. Your job is to keep focus on climbing those stairs – to work out what helps you take steps, and what causes you to take a step down. The more steps you climb, the clearer your energy is. The clearer your energy is, the less is getting in the way of your communication with Spirit.

As you go up steps, you will find there are things your energy invites you to put down, to leave behind on the step. These can be memories, experiences, limited beliefs, and relationships that are not serving you. Take time to explore your options carefully. Listen to how you feel and give yourself permission to let go.

Other steps will offer you snippets of your potential. You will get inspiration, ideas of how you could do things better, and suggestions for changes to make in your life to improve things. Again, take time to explore and open up to that energy. Allow yourself to take what is offered and integrate it into your life.

Sometimes you will find life pushes you down a few steps. That is okay. It is part of the human experience. When you feel ready, just start climbing again.

This is not a race. You are not on a Stairmaster at the gym trying to get the best results as quickly as possible. This is about slow and steady progress, allowing yourself to meet yourself again on each step. Who are you now? How have you changed?

You cannot skip steps. If there are things you need to deal with, you need to find the bravery, commitment, and self-prioritisation to work through it. It is not a target either. You will never reach the top stair where your nonphysical soul resides fully in this physical lifetime. And nor should you! We are here for a human experience, not a soul's one. This is not about bypassing the Earth plane. It is about finding comfort, inspiration, and faith in this space. Climbing this staircase is a lifetime's work. Many lifetimes work!

Understand that Spirit are beside you every single step, always cheering you on and guiding you; but the energy that chooses to step up and out of the current vibration is always and inescapably you.

The Impact on Relationships

One of the things I have noticed that my students (and myself) experience is a changing of relationships brought on by the activities above. It is important to recognise you have chosen this. It is also important to understand that in this universe of free will and choice, you cannot control someone else's energy.

As you climb the metaphorical staircase, the people in your life may not be climbing theirs. Make sure you are patient with those around you. You may suddenly feel that your partner is way more negative, that your best friend is sucking energy from you, or that your work colleagues are disempowered. This is perfectly normal!

You are now experiencing life from the frequency of the step on which you stand. Your thoughts, responses, and emotions are changing as a result. You must not allow others to pull you down onto their steps and sit with them. Never apologise for the steps you have taken. It is hard when you are faced with someone who is feeling helpless, disempowered and angry. (I was that person for a long time.) Your work, as someone undertaking their own Spiritual healing journey, is to hold space for yourself, to be determined, and focused on you.

Your light will shine on those who come into contact with you. If they *choose* so, it can activate the light inside them, inspire them, and motivate them on their own journeys. Equally, if they *choose* not to grow, that is their choice to make. The most important thing is <u>you don't let this stop your own progression</u>.

5
I'm Not Good Enough

Do you find yourself thinking these thoughts about yourself?

- Who am I to connect to the Sprit World? I am just me.
- I am not perfect.
- I am not always "Spiritual".
- I get things wrong.
- I do not know what I'm doing.

Well, here's a newsflash… I do too! This is a big barrier that all of us mediums face. But Spirit say to me:

- Who said you needed to be anything?
- Who put those rules and regulations and unformed ideas into your mind? That you needed to be different somehow, but you are not sure what or how?
- Who told you, you were not good enough?
- The answer: **You did**.

Whether it's life experience that created the continuous thought that you are not good enough, or whether it just popped out of nowhere, it's not Spirit telling you that you can not do it – it is <u>you</u> telling yourself that you can't. The key for mediumistic development is realising this truth and pushing through it. And you will have to push through it again and again and again.

I sometimes worry I am a disappointment to people I meet. I do not fulfil that guru expectation – I am never covered head to toe in a silk kaftan, speaking in proverbs, wafting into a space in a cloud of sage and good intention. You are more likely to find me chugging a lager, cussing profusely, and wearing too much makeup and neon animal print.

I recognize now that I spent so long waiting for Spiritual connection to make me more Spiritual, that I missed a huge chunk of time that I could have just been getting on with it.

You are good enough, <u>right now</u>. Spirit are with you, <u>right now</u>. You are supposed to be enjoying a human experience! You are not here to bypass being who you are so you can preach to a congregation of followers about the ways of Spirit. You are not here to speak in proverbs, on a special mission to be the most Spiritual person that ever lived. You are here to shine, for who you are: Complex, flawed, unapologetically human; Connected, beautiful, and hopeful.

Gifts

In mediumship we have a lot to overcome with this idea of a "gift" – that some people are the lucky ones who can communicate with the Spirit world, but the rest of us cannot. That is what I believed, and I believed it for a long time. But I am here now to say it's poppycock!

Some people have more of an innate ability, yes, but the ability is there for all of us. Think of your ability like a muscle. You need to train it. Work on it. Practice with it. If you wanted to run a marathon tomorrow, you would find that impossible, wouldn't you? But if you had two years to prepare, practice, and get strong, and if you were passionate and committed to it, you could do it! Mediumship is no different. Just as there are some people who are naturally more athletic and would find running easier, there are some people who are just more easily connected to Spirit. However, that does not mean it is unachievable for everyone else.

Mediumistic ability is like singing. Yes, some people are born with a naturally amazing voice that makes the hairs on the back of your neck stand on end. But many great singers have been taught. They have learnt how to use their vocal cords and their lungs to make a beautiful sound to share with the world.

You will have to commit. You will have to push through your own mental barriers and boundaries. You will need to fight the inevitable excuses and show up. I guarantee, Spirit will be there showing up for you.

I believe that we all have the same connection to Spirit. Yep – you have as good as a connection as me. I promise. What stops you connecting in the way I do? It is your own barriers and expectations. You may experience Spirit differently from me, but that does not make it less valid. Your mediumistic journey is about understanding how it works <u>for you</u>.

Activity 5: Powering Up

Powering up is the process of using your thoughts and imagination with intention, to open your energy (open your valves). This makes Spirit communication easier and clearer.

Please note: Once you become accomplished at maintaining an open state, you will no longer need to power up to work with Spirit. I do not sit and meditate in front of an audience before I start work. That would be ridiculous! By doing this practice many, many times over the last decade, I can now open my energy with just a thought.

Here is how you can practice powering up:

Take some long, slow deep breaths. Imagine your energy looking like a snow globe after it has been shaken up, and your energy is moving all around you. To work with Spirit most easily you need to feel that all those noisy, busy energies around you have slowed and stopped. You need the snow to settle. Breathe slowly and steadily until you feel this has happened. It will get quicker with practice.

Now direct your breath into your gut. Connect with that space. Imagine a tiny orb of golden light there. As you breathe into it, it starts to glow brighter and expand. Continue focusing on that space and breathing into it. After a few breaths it becomes a flame. Continuing breathing into that golden flame until it becomes a golden fire. Keep going! Allow that gorgeous healing fire to fill your being. Feel that golden light spreading out of your physical self, and shining all around you, into your aura and beyond. See yourself in your mind's eye. You are shining like a star! How brightly can you make yourself shine? Hold that space for as long as you wish. A couple of minutes is fine to begin with.

When you are finished, just stop this practice. The energy will naturally dissipate. Have a nice drink of water or a short walk outside if you wish. These are examples of grounding your energy, which is the process of connecting our focus back to this physical realm.

Permission

In my experience, much of this Spiritual journey is simply about giving yourself permission to do what you want to. I held myself back for years, waiting for some tangible sign from the Spirit world that they wanted me to do this work. It took me longer than it should have to realise that the fact that I *wanted* to do this work *was* the sign! We often have the idea that the sign will be bigger, stronger, more profound. Really, it's about giving yourself permission to do what you wanted all along. The calling is the desire!

In mediumship, much of Spirit communication is giving yourself permission to accept what is already there. Your doubting mind is important. I believe all great mediums have this voice that pushes you to take your work further and strive for better evidence. In the majority of evidential connections, it is the first thing we pick up on that is right. If we give ourselves permission to just share it, without editing, providing clarification, or holding onto it, our work would be so much easier!

6
Spooky Stuff

Fear can be such a problem for lightworkers. It stops so many of you from following this path because you are afraid of negative energies, entities, and demons. I can only share with you from my own experience here, and that is there is nothing to fear from the Spirit world. There is only love in the Spirit world. There is only light in the Spirit world. I have had such a journey with this, and I would like to share it with you.

Quite early in my journey I trained as an Entity Release Practitioner. I was told by other mediums I had a naturally aptitude for this work, and believed it was the backbone of my future work with Spirit. As an Entity Release practitioner my job was to go out into the world and clear negative energies and attachments from people and their homes. I did this for quite some time. I perceived some really horrible things and felt some very disturbing presences. This work solidified my faith. I could stand in the energy of something very dark, very scary (that at that time I believed was something from the Spirit world) and feel safe and protected. I knew no harm would come to me. For that reason, it was such a gift to me. I built so much trust in my guides and angels, knowing they were there.

We had amazing results with this work. Every home and person I worked with experienced transformational results.

Then, a question formed in my mind. Once it started, it would not stop. I knew I was safe. I knew when I called on Spirit they came instantly. I knew I was clearing energy. I knew that Spirit are clever – far more intelligent than me. Spirit are all-seeing, all-knowing, and all-amazing, more than I can even begin to understand in my reduced human consciousness.

So why did they need me?

If Spirit are all-seeing and all-knowing, why did the angels need me to come into someone's house to direct them to a negative presence that needed dispelling? Why wouldn't they just do it? What could I possibly have in my lower vibrational, human form that Spirit haven't got a better version of? If Spirit have the intelligence that they have shown me time and time again that they do, would they leave a soul trapped here?

My Spirit team brought forward this image of a stupid angel, floating on a cloud saying, "Oh, I can see that human down there, suffering, but I'm not going to do anything to help until another human asks me to." That does not sound like Spirit, does it? The Spirit world I know and love wouldn't leave someone struggling in a situation they have no power over. The Spirit world I know does not leave people behind because of their choices and experiences. The Spirit world I know does not forget about anyone.

Just like a toffee stuck in my teeth, these thoughts would not leave me alone. I now know this was Spirit finding a way to open me up to a new understanding. I spoke to Spirit. I spoke to teachers, shamans, and mediums. I read books. I researched until my brain gave up. I sat with my guides and questioned them. Here is what I found:

- There is nothing to fear in the Spirit world.
- All negative and disharmonious energy is created by humans, sometimes left behind in tragic circumstances or passings.

- We all go to the same place when we experience physical death, regardless of our deeds on earth or any choices we make that lead to our passing.
- Our world is not separate from the Spirit world but contained and immersed within it.

If the negative and horrible energy I had felt and seen in my mind's eye wasn't Spirit, then what was it? Spirit showed me that it is the echo of what has been left behind. Think about someone dying in great physical pain, left alone and suffering. Earth is a physical manifestation of energy. All that has happened is that as they left the physical realm, they left behind all the negative energy they felt. Like a snake shuffling off its skin, as the Spirit went home to their natural state they left everything behind them that could not exist in that space.

The same goes for unhappy experiences and difficult times. When your emotions and your mind are turned to lower vibrational frequencies, you perpetuate more of what you are thinking about. You know this from when you have had a bad day. You woke up tired, unrested, and grumpy. Then, the milk for your morning coffee had turned sour. You stub your toe and smash a glass. There is more negativity. You continue throughout the day with more and more things going wrong, and the negative experience gets bigger.

Imagine this happening over a longer time period. Imagine a couple living in a house where they no longer want to be together. They constantly argue, feeling stressed, immersed in negativity. What happens when they decide to move forward? What do they leave behind? Think of this on an even bigger scale. What could be left behind in so many situations?

Near my home is a place where a young man sadly died on his bike. His parents have left a memorial for him. Every person who drives past that space is reminded of his death, of the sorrow his family feels. Humans are generally ill-equipped to think about death. Many of us are so afraid of it. Now think of all the drivers that go past that space. Some of them do not see it. Some of them think of him and feel sad for him and his family. Some people are spooked by it. Everyone who engages with the memorial leaves a little bit of energetic imprint behind. If you end up with lots of people going past feeling sad and spooked, that energy will start to grow, and eventually can leave something behind that is almost tangible. This is why you sometimes get the heebie-jeebies when you go to old places, or places where you know something bad has happened. It does not mean that the Spirit of the young cyclist is rooted to the place on the side of the road. He is with this family. Why would you linger at the scene of your death when you could be with people you love?

Now think of your own life. Think about when you were tired, felt helpless, unhappy and squashed. You carried a weight of negativity in you and around you. Spirit wanted you to put that down and release it, but you had to allow yourself to do so. What would a psychic have picked up from your energy if they had met you then?

When I was first introduced to Spirit by my friend, Sylvia, I felt sometimes that sitting with her was like sitting in the sun when I had been cold in the shade. It was a completely different frequency.

Consider your valves. If you have turned them open to receive on the spooky setting, you will receive exactly that. You are limiting your energy and experience to receive what you expect. This is why some people find graveyards peaceful and healing while some find them scary and dark. You receive exactly what you allow yourself to receive. If you want to feel

Spirit, you always will because they are always present. However, your expectations can limit how you perceive their energy. Sometimes we are just perceiving energy through our own filter of negative expectation.

People tell stories of the scary things they have experienced. Over time, these stories get embellished and dramatized. Because of the way human memory works, we add to these stories, change them, and yet still believe them to be factually correct. For example, I have a friend who had an experience where her grandfather in Spirit kept moving a photograph of the two of them together. Sometimes it would be placed face down, sometimes it changed in position. I always took this to be him just saying, "Hi," letting her know he was around. I did not see her for several months as we were both busy. When we finally caught up, the story had evolved. Now, there were loud bangs, dramatic sliding effects from the pictures dragging themselves across counters. She was now convinced that she was being haunted. Once I gently dug around the facts of the matter, I realised that nothing different had happened since last time we met. In fact, her grandfather had stopped moving the picture once he realised it was scaring her. So, over time, in her mind, the experience of her grandfather communicating had not physically changed, but her perception of it had. By this time, I was developed enough in my mediumship to be able to connect to him and validate his continued presence in her life. Luckily, she was open to amending her view of the situation and realised it was him after all. This changed her experience of it, and now she wishes her grandfather would once more move those pictures and give her that glorious physical sign she once had from him.

Let us remind ourselves of the way it works. What you expect limits what you can receive. Your expectations control your valves. If your valves are set to negativity, then that is what you will experience, no matter the source of the energy. Your mind will interpret energy through its own filter and its filter is the sum of your experiences and knowledge.

When you are experiencing another human's anguish, pain, sorrow, lack of self-love, and fear, you are experiencing the lowest of vibrations. What does your brain do when it is trying to interpret that energy? Your brain creates a point of reference. For me, that is creatures from horror movies. It does not mean the creatures are there. It just means that my brain is using them as an image to help me understand the energy I am perceiving. When I worked as an Entity Release practitioner, I communicated with what felt like were sentient beings. This was a big barrier to my understanding and releasing what I had previously been taught.

Energy talks, but not with words. Your brain creates words from the energy. In the Spirit world, they do not speak because they do not have voice boxes. Instead, we communicate with energy. You are receiving communication from that Spirit, person, or physical space. You know how you can tell when you walk into a room that someone has had an argument? In that scenario you were receiving that information by feeling it. If you had tried to receive it in words, what would you have received?

We create our own realities. We hear that a lot in terms of the more positive side of manifestation and law of attraction. But this can also apply when you believe you are being haunted, that there is a bad energy around, or someone is watching. I believe that this physical realm has a huge variety of different energy frequencies in it. You tune in to whichever band you choose, either consciously or unconsciously. And you pull energy to you that matches the frequency you are tuned in to. Have you ever watched a horror movie only for there to be a spooky creak on your upstairs landing, a lightbulb blow or the shadowy outline of a man at the end of your bed (who turns out to be a pile of laundry)? You have moved into that vibrational space so you are experiencing the frequency you are at. We are like giant vortexes – pulling energy towards us. Any other day the lightbulb would be a frustration, not a heart stopping trauma, the creak would be the laws of physics, the laundry just a nagging pile of stuff for you to deal with.

It is important to understand the difference. I am not saying spooky stuff does not happen. I am saying that for all the cases I have worked it was either not a Spirit at all and was just energy, or it was a loving Spirit in a moment of desperation, trying to get someone's attention. Humans have low vibrational energy, disharmony, greed, pain and hurt. That is part of the physical incarnation. Spirit are only light and love.

Sometimes Spirit will try to get attention using items in a physical space. Imagine a grandmother in Spirit watching over her granddaughter, wanting her to know she is making a very bad decision. She visits her granddaughter in dreams, stands beside her every day, and sends her healing and encouragement. The grandmother watches her granddaughter failing to open up to her instincts and not accept her healing, all the while wishing her grandmother would give her a sign and support her. If the grandmother had an opportunity to make something physically move to send a signal, don't you think she would? Sometimes, Spirit have to take steps to show they are here. That does not mean they are trying to scare you. They are just trying to get your attention.

Similarly, Spirit can grab your attention through sound. Some people can receive communication from Spirit through clairaudience. Clairaudience is when one hears Spirit as an external force, outside of your own head, in the same way we hear each other. I have only had a couple of true clairaudient experiences in my life. The one example that sticks out to me is when I was driving along a country lane, minding my own business, and I heard a voice shout, "Watch out! Brake now!" I slammed on my brakes and am forever grateful I did. At that moment, a tractor and trailer came fast around the corner on the wrong side of the road, narrowly missing my car. I am convinced that I would no longer be here without that message.

One of the most amusing thoughts I have is the idea of demons coming up to earth to be trapped in Victoriana dolls. I see a lot of mediums spouting this, and it is absolute rubbish. If demons did exist and had the infinite powers of a dark force, and were sent to earth to wreak havoc, can you really imagine choosing to exist inside a stationary object wearing a dress? Couldn't you think of a better way to do this? We find these dolls a little uncomfortable, so we project our fears onto them. And, of course, it is great subject matter for social media "likes"! Profiteering from fear is an age-old practice. Religion used it as a great way to gain followers and earn an income. Some mediums do this now.

Remember that rule from the front of this book about free will and choice? Remember that what you believe, you receive? If you believe you have a Spirit attachment, you will experience what feels like exactly that. If you believe someone is draining your energy, they will. If you believe there are things in the Spirit world who wish to do you harm, you will not feel safe in your practice. The most important thing is that you feel safe. It took me a long time to surrender to Spirit and trust. You need to do what you need to do to feel secure as long as you accept that this is not a true reflection of the Spirit world, but rather has more to do with your own belief system.

The problem for Spirit is that they are with us all the time. If you believe they are going to respond negatively to you, or that there is a low vibration energy around, then your valves are automatically open to only receive that frequency. This can create a self-fulfilling prophecy. When you expect there to be spooky stuff, and you reach out to feel Spirit, you will feel them because they are there. But you will experience only through your filter of expectation that it will be bad! Then, when you feel the bad energy, it will validate your expectation, and the cycle will continue.

You can even call lower vibration energy to you, through your expectations. If you believe you are being haunted you can become like a magnet, drawing negative energy to you, which becomes a very real experience for some people.

If you feel that you want to protect yourself whilst working on this process, then let me recommend an approach that I used to follow. (I must add here that I have not felt the need to protect my home or workspace from Spirit for quite a few years now. I just do not fear the Spirit world. If I did, I would not continue to work with them, in my family home, where my children live.)

Protection Invocation (Note: This can be spoken out loud or said in your head)

I ask Archangel Michael and his legions of angels to place me in a dome of protection. I set my intention to work only with energies of the highest vibrations available to me at this time. I ask my Guides, Angels, and Helpers to secure this space and watch over me while I work. Thank you. Thank you. Thank you.

The key here is comfort. You do not want to be worried about negative energies when you need to be focusing on the high vibrational ones. So, do what you need to do to make yourself comfortable. Spirit never judge. They will always give you what you need to be able to work with them.

Activity 6: Clearing Your Home

As your vibration starts to rise, you may find your home starts to feel heavy or incompatible with you. It is important to remember that it is you that has changed, not your home!

Start with one room at a time. Sit in the room and power up as described in a previous activity. Ask your Spirit Team to assist, direct, and inspire you. Just the thought is enough.

Look around the space. Is there anything that needs to go? Is there clutter you are not using? Are there things that you do not like but you forgot were there?

How does the room feel? Does anything need moving? Do any spaces feel dark or congested? Open the window. Light a candle in the dark space, place a crystal there, or put a light on. Maybe burn some incense if you have some. Room sprays are great too!

Ask any energy that is not in alignment with you to leave the space immediately. Imagine it flowing out of the room and to the outdoors where nature will rebalance it.

This simple method works wonders. Clear the whole house one room at a time.

You can also raise the vibration of your home even further! Play your favourite music (loudly)! Dance! Sing! Laugh!

Clearing your space is such an important part of your development. The energy you surround yourself with can massively impact your own vibration, just as your vibration can impact your space. Think of it like a staircase on your set of stairs. There is a limit to how much further you can go without working out how to undo that childproof lock and get through the barrier.

Space clearing also helps you to physically experience the newness of you. Imagine you have a painting on the wall that you no longer like, one that you bought when you were 20 steps below where you are now. Think of that painting like a lower frequency and a constant reminder of a time now past. The opposite can also be true. If there is something you still love but holds the energy of the past, you can use it to remind you of how far you have come.

This exercise is a real mix of physical act to shift energetic frequency. Every time I go through an energetic shift, I find myself clearing out cupboards and rooms, decorating, and moving furniture. As physical creatures, we replicate our internal experience externally (and vice versa).

Feel stuck? Move your body! Feel congested? Clear out a cupboard! Feel uninspired? Decorate! You will be amazed at the difference it makes.

I want to finish this chapter with a story that shows exactly what we are on about!

When I was first developing, my sister came to my home one evening. I was telling her about my experiences in my development circle. Her little Chihuahua started barking, staring intensely across the room at the space in front of the window. He would not stop. My sister mentioned how it "was just like someone was stood there," and we started to get spooked. The hairs were standing up on the back of my neck. I started thinking about the graveyard opposite my home. Who was this visitor? Were they malevolent? I took a deep breath and said, "Spirit, whoever you are, you are scaring us. Please go away." The dog instantly stopped barking. That was worse! What had he seen that we could not? My poor sister even had to accompany me to the toilet because I was too scared to go alone.

The following week, I met with my development circle. As we were getting ready to work and sitting in the energy, my teacher fixed her eyes on me. She said, "Hannah, why did you tell your Granny to go away this week?" I was mortified. Granny. She was the sweetest, kindest, most loving lady that ever lived, and I had told her to go away! Lesson learned.

7
How it Works

By now, we have established that we are all part of the Spirit world, yes? And we are communicating with our own Spirit all the time, aren't we? So how do we communicate with the separate beings that are with us, guiding and loving us? Well, the first thing I want you to remember is that our connection with Spirit is a natural state. I know I have already said this, but I am going to keep saying it again and again because this is by far the biggest hurdle for all developing mediums.

You are, right now, a soul encased in a physical body. At the same time, your soul maintains a presence in the Spirit world. Also, your soul is a unique entity, but it always remains part of the oneness of the Spirit world and the oneness with the Creator (God, Source etc.). Because of this, we are all connected. Every single human on this planet and every single soul in the Spirit world are connected.

When I say communicating with Spirit is a natural state, it is because you are trying to communicate with something you are already part of. Yes, you can make it easier and clearer by working on your vibration and shifting your frequency, but you are already doing it.

The way Spirit show it to me is like the waves on the sea. The waves are individual, but they are also part of the whole ocean. A murkier part of the sea is still part of the sea, even if some parts shine with aquamarine brilliance. Even if you feel that you are murky, it does not mean you are going to feel like that forever!

We are physical beings trying to communicate with the nonphysical beings that surround us. What does it mean to be nonphysical? Well, for a start, it means the Spirit is no longer in a human body. When I "see" a Spirit, I see them as a light, sometimes human-shaped, but more often as a pillar of moving light, like a flame. The lack of a human body means the Spirits you are communicating with no longer have a voice box. Spirit are not literally talking to us mediums – they are *communicating* with us using energy. Lots of mediums, myself included, liken it to playing energetic charades.

We can communicate with different forms of Spirit: Our Spirit guides, our loved ones in Spirit, our angels, our higher selves and even those enlightened beings known as ascended masters (for example, Jesus, and the Buddha).

Our Spirit guides are like a team of cheerleaders, just for you. They are teacher energies who love you more than anything and who know your potential and the best way to get you where you need to be to experience that potential. They bring encouragement, wisdom, support, and a lot of humour. They can present in human form, but also as animals, lights, aliens, and even plants! I have received messages from guides brought in on the wind blowing through trees and in clouds in the sky. You just need to keep an open mind.

Our loved ones in Spirit are the people you have met and known in your physical life, but who have moved into the Spirit world. They are also the people you have not met, such as great-great-grandparents, who watch over and love you too. They bring support and encouragement and help us work through the process of physical death and reach an understanding that they are still beside us.

Angels are higher vibrational beings that bring a stronger, clearer energy. Although they can involve themselves with specific and personal issues, their approach tends to be for the greater good of the whole, rather than on an individual basis.

Our higher selves are the parts of our soul that remain connected to the Spirit world. It is a multifaceted, many-levelled brilliance contained in your human shell, but it is not your whole soul. If the entirety of your soul tried to place itself in your human physical body, you would not be able to function. We are limited in our physical form by our consciousness, which serves a purpose – we are here to experience the physical world, not the Spirit world.

Ascended masters are Spirit that lived a human life but have now moved into a more enlightened state. They vibrate at a higher frequency. They are great energies to work with because they bring wisdom, teachings, and guidance from the divine, but they also understand the trials and tribulations of the human experience.

The Clairs

If you are interested in mediumship development (and I hope you are, if you are reading this book!) you will probably have heard of the clairs. If you haven't, here is a brief explanation for you:

The clairs are the ways that we humans receive and interpret information energy. They include:

Clairvoyance – seeing energy

- Clairaudience – hearing energy
- Claircognizance – knowing energy
- Clairalience – smelling energy
- Clairgustance – tasting energy
- Clairsentience – feeling energy

Now that you know them, I want you to forget them! We humans love our labels and limitations, don't we? Talking about clairs is a useful way of opening up to how you may receive communications, relating them to senses that are familiar to human body.

When I meet with new students for the first time, many like to start by telling me instantly which clair they use to interpret energy. In response, I tell them that what they are doing is putting a limit on what they can receive. If you say you only *see* Spirit, then that is the only valve that is open for you. It gives the Spirit world no other option than to work with you that way. If you remain open to all ways of receiving, then more valves are clear and ready to work!

It is my belief that when we are working with Spirit, it is a collaboration. I have heard it said that Spirit control how we receive the information from them, but I think it's a mixture of us and them. We have valves that are open or closed, and Spirit are aware of which is which. Spirit, with their infinite intelligence and understanding, send us communications through the best available open valve. I also think that sometimes our brains control how we perceive the energy we are receiving and use our memories, knowledge, and prior experiences to make the closest available match.

You hear mediums speak of "seeing" a Spirit or "hearing" a Spirit, but for the most part, this experience is within the construct of the mind. By "seeing" they mean they are receiving the energy as an image in their mind. By "hearing" they mean they are receiving the energy as words, but in their mind.

The 5 Frequencies

There are many ways that we can work to receive and perceive energy. It is crucial that you know the difference. Think of yourself as a radio, receiving whatever station or frequency you are tuned into. I teach five different ways (frequencies) to work with energy:

- **Psychic Frequency.** Working with psychic frequency is tuning into the energy of someone, or something in this physical, Earthly realm. Psychic is energy to energy interpretation. This occurs when you are reading my energy or aura, and when you are reading the energy of a room, a crystal, a photo, or an object. This energy is always in this physical space. It is not the frequency used for communicating with the realm beyond. Psychic detectives communicate with the energy of a space, or the energy a person has left behind. They filter energy through the intention of the answers they are seeking. Auragraphs and card readings are often carried out in the psychic frequency, but sometimes mediums will also ask for guidance to support the reading in the Spirit Guide frequency, too.

- **Spirit Guide Frequency.** When we work in the Spirit Guide frequency we are altering our energy to be able to receive guidance, instruction and support from our team of helpers in the spirit world. This frequency is not just limited to Spirit guides, but also includes ascended masters and angels too.

- **Healing Frequency.** When working with the healing frequency, you are opening as a channel to bring in beautiful, high vibrational energy from the universe and into someone's energy system. Your awareness remains in this psychic space (Earthly realm) but the energy you transfer comes from the Spirit world. Think of this modality as using energy to move someone up steps on their metaphorical staircase.

- **Evidential Mediumship Frequency.** Working in the evidential mediumship means altering your energy to connect with the souls of loved ones who are no longer in the physical space. Evidential mediums learning to receive and perceive specific information to prove life after death.

- **Trance Frequency.** When working in trance, you are allowing the Spirit world to assume a certain level of control over your physical self. This frequency is the strongest and deepest blend with the Spirit world that is available to us humans. Trance can be used for Spirit to speak using our voice boxes and heal others. It is also associated with physical phenomena such as transfiguration, which is seeing a physical Spirit apparition on a human body. I have seen female mediums sprout moustaches, people change race and age, noses grow, and glasses appear on the ends of noses. Amazing, isn't it?

I believe that you need to develop every one of these frequencies to be a good, well-rounded medium. Too many focus on just one aspect, but they all play a part.

I have encountered mediums who believe they are working with Spirit, when in fact, they are working psychically. Let me explain. If you are going to see a medium, you will start to think about who you might like to hear from. You might even take a walk down memory lane. As you think about your loved one in Spirit, you might remember how they looked, think about their passing, remember their home, and think of happy memories you shared. This remembrance brings all of that information into your energy field. A psychic would then be able to tell who you want to hear from and even evidential information about this person just from reading your energy, without necessarily connecting to a Spirit at all.

I once saw a medium who told me that my grandmother wanted to talk about me painting a room. This was true. I was decorating. But what did I really want? I wanted to feel the presence of my grandmother once more and to be reunited with her love. For me, true evidential mediumship brings the presence, the healing connection, the hope, and the support. An audience should all be able to feel it, even if the message is not for them.

I do not think mediums work intentionally in the wrong frequency. It just happens that way when the medium does not know better. As a developing medium, it is so important you know the difference. Think of it this way – receiving advice from a fellow human comes from a completely different perspective than advice from the Spirit world.

A friend of mine's sister, Rebecca, went for a reading with another medium. She wanted to hear from her father. That medium instantly said they had Dad present. The medium then proceeded to explain that Dad was warning Rebecca that her husband was cheating on her with another woman. Rebecca was devastated. She had been worried something was happening, and now her beloved father was telling her from the other side she was right all along.

Except the medium was wrong. He was *not* cheating.

The medium was working psychically. Because they were reading Rebecca's energy and not blending with the Spirit world, they had experienced Rebecca's need to hear from her father and her concerns her partner was cheating from the same source: Rebecca. Sadly, the medium did not know the difference, and I am sure they would feel terrible to know they had misled Rebecca. When Rebecca's husband contacted me for help, we managed to unpick the reading and understand what had happened. That could have been such a damaging situation if we had not managed to rectify it.

I also had a client who was told by a medium that their mother wanted them to know their partner was their soul mate. This was shocking to her, as she was making plans to leave him. He was abusive, and she was scared for her children. As a result of that medium's reading, she stayed in that abusive relationship for a further three years. I do not believe that Spirit will ever deliver a message like that. If you recall the rules of Spiritual connection at the beginning of this book, being told that you should stay with someone does not honour your free will and choice.

This is why I am so stalwart in my approach to the frequencies. Not only does it help you to know which frequency you are working in and where the information is coming from, but it ensures that your sitters are getting what they have asked for.

Blending

Whatever frequency you are working in, you are learning to blend with energy and use your natural abilities to understand and interpret that energy. The more you practice the easier this becomes. Imagine blending like two discs of colour: one red one blue. Your energy is the red disc. The energy you are working with (human, Spirit guide or loved one in Spirit) is the blue disc. As you open your valves and start to perceive that energy, the two discs start to touch. As you become more adept at the experience, the discs start to merge. A full blend with the energy would give you one purple disc. (I do not believe that a blend of 100% is actually possible because our humanness won't allow it. Also, aiming for 100% is only going to disappoint you. When I am really "cooking on gas," fully blended with Spirit and getting some amazing evidence, I am only at about 80%.)

Do not set yourself the impossible task of maintaining (or even achieving) that solid purple disc. The more you practice, the more those two discs will blend, and the more easily you will find yourself able to create that blend. At the beginning, your imposter syndrome will say to you that you are making it up, that it is your imagination. That is okay! I expect it was already piping up from Activity 1. At the beginning of your development, the experience might well be 98% you and 2% Spirit. That is still pretty amazing. Wow! You are actually communicating with Spirit! As time passes and you practice more and more, it will become less you and more Spirit. It is a journey.

Flow

The key with mediumship is to deliver the information you have at that moment while you are also receiving the next piece of information. This creates a flow. The more of a flow you are in, the more blending can take place. The stronger the blend, the more of a flow you will, and so on and so forth. It will take you a while to be able to do this. In the meantime, it does not invalidate your experience or the messages you are receiving. It is important for you to understand where you are aiming for!

Intention

Intention is all about choosing the frequency we are tuning into. I like to imagine an old-style radio. I mentally turn my dial into the frequency I want to use. Some people flick mental switches. Others use colour. If you prefer, you can simply state the frequency you want to work in (even as a thought). Saying in your mind, "I am working in the psychic frequency," is enough. Do whatever works best for you.

You may find at the beginning you slip between frequencies, and that is okay. When you realise you are in the wrong energy, just set your intention back to where you want to be. Eventually you will be able to feel the difference between the frequencies and know you are comfortably where you want to be. This takes time and (you have guessed it) practice.

The Blackboard

The blackboard (chalkboard if you are overseas) metaphor was given to me by Spirit a few years ago and has really helped me understand the difficulties we face when working with Spirit. I want you to imagine your energy like a giant blackboard. Written all over it, with brightly coloured chalks, and in writing of different sizes, is everything that is going on with you at the moment. Your blackboard contains:

- Your to-do list
- Your worries
- Your thoughts stream (sometimes overwriting what was already written, sometimes staying put on the board and taking up space)
- Your doubts
- Your memories

When you want to communicate with Spirit, you are asking them to write on your blackboard. (Of course, it may not be written when you experience it, it will be through the clairs.) How clearly Spirit can write on your blackboard depends on how much space they have, and the quality of the chalk provided. Think of the blackboard as your energy, emotions, and mind. Think of the chalk as the vibrational state you are in. How much space do Spirit have to write right now in this moment? What can you do to improve the quality of your chalk?

Activity 7: Blackboard Maintenance

Wouldn't it be lovely if our blackboards could be cleared just by asking? If we could get the best bit of chalk ever manufactured with intention? The above will help, but Spirit are all about empowerment and self-improvement – they will not do it for you!

Take a clean sheet of A4 paper (or 8.5 x 11 for my American friends) and settle your energy.

Write out what is on your blackboard. What is on your mind? As you write down one piece of information, what follows? What thoughts are intruding? What is on your to-do list? What are you worried about? Keep adding to it again and again and again. Follow your instincts. Write some things bigger when you feel drawn. Allow yourself to become the flow of energy.

Stay with it for at least half an hour (set a timer).

When you are done look back at it:

- What is an easy to-do list item you can cross off your board today (e.g., making your optician appointment, replying to that email, etc.)?
- What is just noise that is out of your control (e.g., the results of your blood test, whether your child will pass their exams, etc.)?
- What can you clear off your blackboard easily and what shouldn't be taking space up on it to begin with?

A simple method for releasing things that should be long gone, such as guilt for an argument many years ago, or something said to you that hurt your feelings, is to imagine it like a balloon in your hand. Release the string and let it go. This simple practice helped me to remember to release. There really is no value in holding onto things from the past that no longer serve a purpose. I would be sitting there all clogged up, beating myself up for the bum note I hit in karaoke three months ago, rather than focusing on my potential and the future.

For more emotionally reactive things, it is great practice to sit with them. Feel the memory. Feel your response. Remember your reaction. I like to pretend I am videoing a journal and speak my memories into being. Some people prefer writing things down in a journal, others channel this into art. Experiment and find what works for you.

For some of the bigger, more emotional things, I wholeheartedly recommend counselling. Someone holding a space for you to express how you really feel can be such an empowering experience.

Your blackboard is _never_ fully clear. As someone living a human life, things are constantly being added to it, and that is okay. You just need a space for Spirit to write upon it, even if it is tiny writing. Remember, the more space available on your blackboard, the bigger Spirit can write. The bigger they can write, the easier it is to receive the information and feel their presence. Some days, your blackboard will be so full with writing from your day-to-day life that it would be foolish to even worry about asking Spirit to write. Just go with the flow and find your own personal balance. Some days you will need a push to clear that board, some days it will be naturally emptier, and some days you would be crazy to even try!

Doing The work

Whatever frequency you are working in, we call the experience of interpreting and understanding energy a "reading." Whether you have someone sat opposite you who is looking for information and guidance, or you are working alone connecting to your Spirit team, you are doing a reading. You are either reading for yourself or reading for others.

Nothing beats practice. It really does make perfect. The more practice you do, the more you are able to experience energy, and experience it more quickly. The more you can experience, the deeper your blend. The deeper your blend, the more information you will be able to receive. The more you receive that is validated, the more you will believe. The more you believe, the deeper your blend, and so on!

8
The Psychic Frequency

As I described above, working with the psychic frequency is tuning into the energy people, places, or things in the physical, Earthly realm. includes things like people, places, and things. For example:

- You read my energy.
- I read your energy.
- You read the energy of a room, a crystal, an aura, a photo, or a someone's personal belonging.

I believe that we are all using our psychic abilities all the time. It is a natural frequency for us. However, psychic frequency does not involve communicating with those who have moved into the Spirit world.

Most people who are drawn to mediumship have very strong, natural psychic abilities. Often, these individuals may experience other people's emotions and physical ailments. People with these abilities are frequently referred to as "empaths." As an empath myself, I felt from a young age that everyone else's moods and feelings were somehow my responsibility. Several adults, who were dealing with their own issues, leaned on me for support when I was really too young to provide the guidance they needed. For example, when I was 14 years old, I worked in a café. The owner of the venue was having an affair with a married man. She would often come to work and cry to me about his refusal to leave his family. Although I was way too immature to deal with carrying the weight of her emotional burden, I took it on and tried to help because I could feel her pain and sadness. As a result, not only did I offer support when she openly needed me to, I overcompensated on a general level. I became a people-pleaser. I tried to make her laugh. I shielded her from difficult customers. I would not take breaks or ask for help when I needed it. I always said, "Yes," to every demand and every moment. I am sure you have similar memories of experiences like this. It seems to be a common occurrence for those on the spiritual development path.

Again, it is important to remember that you are in control of what you receive and perceive. If you are an empath and need to guard yourself from being drawn too far into other's emotions, just image yourself in an impenetrable ball of light and setting your intention not to feel others' energy. You may just need to keep reminding yourself because your years of conditioning will override your intention. Knowing that it is not your job to carry other people's emotional burden can really help. Once Spirit showed me that I have to let people fall, fail, and feel for their own development, it freed me up to focus on my own.

Spirit showed me my son as a baby, learning to take his first steps. When he would wobble and fall down, I would not sweep in, pick him up and carry him. If I had done that, I would now be trying to manoeuvrer a 6ft 3 being around the world! I knew that he needed to learn to walk to function, so instead of trying to fix it for him I encouraged him through the wobbles, the shock of his newly discovered legs letting him down and the practice needed to become a toddler. I stayed at the sidelines, arms open wide, cheering him on. The learning journey for us all (even as adults) is the same. True belief in someone is not taking away their lessons and learning, but supporting them through the experiences.

When we receive energy psychically, we still perceive it through the clairs. This is why a strong psychic ability can help with your mediumship because it is all about understanding how you receive and interpret energy. You are building your own encyclopaedia of understanding, including your own language for energy. And you will spend the rest of this lifetime adding to it.

I find psychic one of the easier frequencies to sit in because it remains in this physical vibrational space. When we want to communicate with the Spirit world, we have to alter our energy to be able to blend with them. Because psychic work is carried out on the frequency we already exist in, it is less draining to be in that space. Plus, we often already use our psychic abilities on a daily basis. As a result, it is easier to hold that frequency, and less tiring to be in it. Psychic and Spirit Guide frequencies are also generally a more positive energy because you are opening someone up to their own potential, giving them guidance and inspiration. When you are doing an evidential reading, you are typically immersed in someone's sadness. It is transformational to be able to prove that we continue past physical death, but you are still sitting in the space of someone's grief and loss, which is a lower vibrational energy.

The downside to the psychic frequency being more comfortable and more familiar is that you may subconsciously move into psychic without meaning to. This can happen especially at the beginning of your practice when you are seeking validation from your sitters. To help prevent this from happening, it is important to become familiar with how the psychic frequency feels compared to the others. This takes time and lots of practice. At the beginning of your unfoldment, it is completely normal not to feel a difference between the frequencies. However, professional mediums should be able to feel the difference, and also be able to feel which frequency other mediums are in when they are working.

The reason why the distinction is critical is because it is important for a sitter to know the source of the information and guidance they are receiving. Advice coming directly from Spirit holds more gravitas that advice from a human being. Spirit only want to open someone up to their fullest potential. They do not give a list of instructions. As humans we are limited by our belief system, experiences, tastes and understanding. We need to recognise and understand our own limitations and how it can impact the readings and guidance we deliver.

The psychic frequency is great for:

- Working out areas of congested energy, and understanding what has caused that congestion in the first place
- Feeling into your own energy to work out what your body/emotions/brain needs from you
- Understanding someone's worries or what is holding them back
- Acknowledging the work that needs to be done
- Feeling and lighting up someone's potential
- Helping someone to heal
- Understanding the need of someone who has come for a reading
- Checking if your animal friends are okay
- Asking your plants what they need

- Assessing stagnant energy in your home and making changes for a better flow
- And so much more!

The psychic frequency it also useful for seeing energy that is coming in. However, it is not advisable for future predictions because, mostly, the future is not set in stone. **We create our path as we walk along it**. As a psychic you do sometimes get specific pieces of information about someone's future, but you also become aware of huge amounts of potential energy, often with a feeling accompanying it of what the sitter needs to do to allow this energy to manifest, and how long that takes is entirely up to them!

Often people expect mediums to be like the caricature you see of a fortune teller, gazing into a crystal ball with a list of instructions for future happiness – "wait for the clock to strike 12 on the 5th June and look for the man with the yellow tulip". This is not how it works, and if you are ever unlucky enough to be in front of someone who is making these kinds of statements I would be very wary. There are certain elements of our lives that are decided before we get here, but these are few and far between. For the most part our decisions, our energy and our choices decide the next step in the journey. When working psychically you might feel or see future events for someone, but these are not guaranteed. It is important to recognise that we can take steps to change the outcome. We are not being pushed along a path without choosing. We are making our experiences happen as we go.

A great example of this is a complaint I received from someone who had come for a reading, we'll call her Susan. She was looking for love and hopeful that a new relationship was on its way. I told Susan that I could see the potential for a relationship, but that she needed to work hard on her self-love to change her own vibration (we can only receive from the Universe that which is compatible with our own energy) and then she would need to put herself out of her comfort zone by joining new groups and expanding her social circle in order to cross paths with her potential love match. Susan pushed for a timescale, she'd been on her own for many years and was ready for a change. I told her that depending on the work she did on herself she could have it within 6 months. 7 months later my email pinged with a message from her, she was frustrated, I'd promised her a relationship – where was it? Some gentle probing showed that Susan hadn't done any of the self-love work I'd suggested, she'd managed to keep it up for just two days before forgetting about it. And, unsurprisingly, she'd not joined any groups like I'd advised either. She'd sat at home, in the same vibrational energy, not changing anything and then felt I'd let her down because what she wanted hadn't manifested into her life like a wish from a fairy godmother. I told her the potential remained the same – it was available to her IF she did as was advised, or found another path with the same energetic outcome, but the work needed was immovable!

Activity 8: Psychic Blending

Start by powering up as described in earlier Activity, above. You should have had plenty of practice as this, and can now feel when you are empowered and energised. Your blackboard has a space on which the energy can write! This should only take a couple of long, slow breaths.

Set your intention (dial in your radio) to the psychic frequency. Look around the space in which you find yourself. Is there an object or an area that catches your eye? Feel into it. What impressions do you get? What emotions arise within you? Does it feel positive or negative? If it was a colour, what colour would it be? Why? What vibration does it hold? Are you receiving words? Smells? Sounds? Feelings? Pictures? Knowing? All of the above?

Activity 9: Psychic Work with a Living Being

This activity can be carried out on an animal, a plant, or a tree. It is best to try this activity with a plant or tree to begin with. Animals have an irritating habit of feeling your energy approach and moving away!

Allow your energy to settle and your power to build. Feel into your aura (the space that surrounds your physical self, but that is part of your energy body). If your aura was a colour what colour would it be? Imagine that colour surrounding you like a big bubble. With every breath you take deepen that colour as your energy expands.

Take a quick "taste" of your subject's energy (the tree/plant/animal/human). What colour is its/their aura? Note: Auras are made up of multiple colours, this is purely for the visualisation to help the connection.

Now, send your energy like a stream of coloured light to your subject. Imagine your colours swirling and blending with theirs.

Relax into this blending experience. What impressions are you picking up from them? What are you feeling? What are you seeing? What are you knowing? Can you put this experience into words?

Do not be afraid to check your findings where you can. If you feel that the animal is sad, is there a reason you can see? If you feel like the plant wants to be in the sun, can you move it? When you check back, does it feel better?

Practice holding this blending for as long as you are able. Start small and work your way up, I recommend beginning with 5 minutes and building your strength over time.

I also recommend recording your findings in your notebook, as a voice note, or as a video. A massive part of development is learning to translate energetic experience into words. The sooner you start this practice, the better!

My students often ask me, "If working psychically isn't communicating with Spirit, then what is the point?" There are many benefits! Psychic readings can

- Open a sitter up to their potential.
- Help a sitter understand where they are experiencing blockages or low vibrational energy in their body or aura.
- Give a sitter validation about what they are feeling.
- Give someone a boost of energy.
- Give someone permission to do what they want to do.
- Inspire and educate and
- Keep people heading in the right direction ("Don't give up!" "I can feel it coming in for you." "Just a little more!").

9
The Healing Frequency

When I talk about "healing," I am referring to the process of intentionally accepting a higher vibrational energy into your energy system. This energy works on your whole self (mind, body, and Spirit) and it knows where and how best to work with you. This is what is meant by "holistic healing," or, if you will, "whole-istic healing" – healing *all* of you. You work in collaboration with this power to clear your energy and elevate your frequency. Healing is not a case of a magic wand, wiping away anything that needs to go. Instead, it is about inspiring you to give yourself what you need, releasing that which is done, and making choices that support your health and wellbeing.

When you are working with healing, you are inviting a higher vibrational energy into your system. To rise to that level, you need to clear and align your energy to its frequency. You work over time with increasing amounts of the energy from the next step to bring your frequency in line with it. Once you have done enough work, like a hot air balloon freed from its weights, you will rise. Then, begin the process again!

Healing can work on your emotions. It can help you to face what is rising within you, listen to how you feel, and make changes to support your future happiness in your life. Healing can work on your physical body. It can help alleviate discomfort, bring comfort, and rest weary bones. Although I believe very much that your soul is always well, aligned, and in perfect harmony, healing can help with the human part of our Spirit by energising us, thereby releasing congestion and stagnant energy.

I do not believe Spiritual healing is a fix-all. For some of us, our soul contracts (agreements made by our souls for us to have certain experiences in our lifetimes) dictate that health complaints & traumatic experiences are part of our journey here on Earth. However, working with healing energy can lessen the impact of these complaints and help us to navigate difficult times.

There are many different types of healing available including Reiki energy healing, acupuncture, touch therapy, and crystal healing, to name a few. They all work with the same concept that ailments are caused by imbalances in your energy. Creating a flow of higher vibrational energy around your system helps clear blocks and stagnant energy. Holding a supportive space for you to release what you need to helps you feel better and brighter.

People love to overcomplicate the concept of "healing energy" and create a hierarchy for something that is incredibly powerful yet simple. I believe that there is an infinite amount of healing energy in the universe. I also believe that this energy is available to all. How do we access this amazing energy? With intention. We just ask to receive it and it comes in.

Even though it is so simple, we humans created complicated procedures, rules, and regulations because it helps us feel like we are in control. But healing energy is there for you, really! Do we really believe in a Spirit world that would withhold help from someone seeking healing simply because they or the person they are working with has not attended a workshop and received a certificate from another human? I hope not!

"But Hannah," I can hear you ask, "don't you teach Reiki?" I do and I love it. But I do not believe that healing is only available to those who have a Reiki qualification, and I believe that Reiki only opens you up to an energy that is already available to you. A Reiki course is a great way to learn more about healing and how it works, but it is not the only way to access healing energy.

I also strongly recommend you have a session (or sessions!) with a healer. There is something in surrendering to someone else to perform the activity on you that makes it a truly profound experience. I also want you to find the healer that is right for you – you need the experience to be aligned with you and your energy, you should enjoy it, and feel safe and relaxed.

I view healing energy as a high vibrational energy with its own intelligence. For me, it comes from the Spirit world to us to help us open up to our potential, to clear lower vibrational energy, and strengthen your connection to self and to Spirit. This energy will flow into your physical, emotional, and mental energy fields. Because it is intelligent, it knows where best to go for maximum benefit. It knows the order in which you should receive it. It knows how much or how little to give you at any time.

The interesting thing with healing is that often physical discomfort is a sign of a mental or emotional imbalance. For example, it may be confusing for someone who has knee pain feel the energy instead flow into their heart. However, the Spirit world will know that the sore knee is connected to a fear of stepping forward and making change, which results from a lack of self-prioritisation, which in turn comes from a lack of self-love. In this case, Spirit know to direct to healing energy to the real source of the issue, the heart. It is very clever!

You can expect healing energy over time to refine your behaviour, thoughts, vibration, and mental patterns. But healing energy, like all energy, will only obey free will and choice. Think of it like this: You are a smoker with a lung condition and you visit a healer. You receive a wonderful healing session, you see lights, colours, and you feel the energy flowing into you It's an amazing experience. And yet, when you leave, you light a cigarette. You can't then expect the healing to magically cure all your ailments. You might find that over time you naturally start to reduce your intake of cigarettes and make healthier choices. Equally, if you <u>choose</u> to ignore that desire rising within you, that is your right to do so. Spirit won't come along and blow your cigarette out until you get the message. We live in a universe of free will!

The same concept applies to the people in our lives that we know are bad for us. Spirit will not take away the lesson by removing those relationships from us. That is your decision to make. Spirit will not force those people to make better choices, either. But working with healing energy over a long period of time will help you realise that the relationship isn't good for you, and you will decide to take steps to rectify it.

When I open up to healing energy, I visualise it as a flow of golden, sparkling light. This flow is directly from Source and it is infinite. You can never consume too much, nor can you reduce the supply available to others for their own.

Because we work in a universe of free will, you cannot send healing energy to someone else who has not asked for it. They must decide to seek healing for themselves. Many healers forget this, and with the best intentions send healing to others as if they are doing them a favour. If the healing energy is infinite and around us all, what could the healer possibly do that Spirit cannot? If someone is not ready to accept healing for themselves and make the required changes in their life, that is their choice and not someone else's to make it for them.

Just set your intention, ask for it and that beautiful healing energy is coming in. Instantly! I believe the energy flows from the part of us that is eternal and connected to Spirit and out, to where it needs to go, whether that is mind, emotions, body etc. Because the soul is always in perfect alignment and in contact with the Spirit world, we just connect with that space through thought, ask, and the energy starts to flow.

Traditionally, healing energy is perceived as travelling in through the tops of our head, and out through the palms of our hands. If that is how it works for you, that is brilliant! It will always work for you regardless of how you interpret it. Just rest your hands gently on your body where you feel drawn.

For me, healing energy flows in through my heart centre, in the middle of my chest. This is where I always visualise my soul to be. As soon as I ask for healing energy, I can feel the space in my hear centre expand. I imagine it like a physical heart, pumping the energy around my body. I also see it like a light, projecting beautiful healing from source out of my heart, in stages through my physical body, and into my aura. As that healing energy starts to work, I can feel physically where I am holding on to low vibrational energy or emotion. I simply acknowledge it and allow it to gently be cleared by the light. Sometimes I visualise it as a gap or a shadow, and I just gently breathe the healing light into that space and it clears.

A healing session for me can last anywhere from ten to forty-five minutes, and sometimes longer if I fall asleep! I love to play my favourite music in headphones and cocoon myself away from the world. This is my time.

I view healing energy as a higher vibrational energy than where I am right now. Taking the staircase analogy from earlier in this book, you start on a step and the Spirit world know which step is available to you in your progression. They will never give you more than you can handle, more than is healthy for you to receive, or allow you to bypass by jumping twenty steps in one go! Imagine you are on step 4. Spirit know the next step for you is 6, but you need to work through some stuff on step 5 before you can sit comfortably on step 6. You will get step 5 energy first so you can work through it!

Healing energy is received differently at different times. Sometimes you will physically feel it, sometimes you will see it in your mind's eye, sometimes you will see colours, and other times you will feel nothing at all! All is as it should be. Just trust in the experience!

Spirit show healing to me like using a sponge. At the beginning, you are not used to receiving the healing. Like a dry sponge under a tap, most of the energy will roll off and not be absorbed. But if you practice and stick at it, you will find your ability to absorb it grows and grows. This means if you do not feel much of a benefit at first it does not mean you are doing anything wrong. It just means you need to keep at it.

As you work with healing you may find you are more sensitive to things that lower your vibration. It is important for you to keep checking in with yourself to see how you're feeling and giving yourself what you need. For example:

- Want to say, "No"? Say it!
- Want to cancel plans? Do it!
- Want some space? Make it!
- Want some sleep? Allow it!

You may also find events and memories from the past coming up in your thoughts. This is perfectly normal! It is your energy showing you what needs to be released. Spend some time sitting with yourself, remembering what you have been through, who you were, and recognise your growth since then. Forgive yourself for not knowing or doing better, and release it if you can, recognising that for some experiences and traumas we may need to talk it through with a therapist.

After my first healing sessions, I would find events from the past rising in my memories. I felt tricked by the healing. I thought I was supposed to feel better, not remember a past experience that caused me pain. But Spirit guided me to understand the process better. In sitting with the memory, reliving it, forgiving myself and forgiving others, I was able to let go of the energy associated with the memory, and truly heal. Healing is not about ignoring; it is the practice of integrating ourselves and our lessons.

It is important to understand that healing is not always linear. Rather than a smooth line rising to an enlightened state it can be more like a corkscrew. When you work on your healing, you revisit whatever situation needs attention. Once complete, you believe you have put it past you, and you move to the next element. After some time, you find you have circled back to the first issue. You thought you had healed that – why is it back again?! Is this healing broken?! You will find that as you expand in awareness and understanding, your soul will invite you to revisit past situations again from your newly developed perspective. This may happen multiple times. This approach helps you fully integrate the lessons and the understanding for your development.

A personal example of healing for me is being a natural performer. At primary school I participated in weekly assemblies for my entire school, teaching them about history, performing little skits about being a better person, sharing education I had decided was important, and (dear God) I even sang a few times. The melodies of Michael Jackson's "Man in the Mirror" and "Heal the World" were played upon entrance and exit from the hall and I loved it. As I got older my classmates started to bully me. I learned to feel a lot of shame about these events. Students mocked me for years and I wished I had never done any of these assemblies. I started to hide my light and apologise for being so out there. It was only in sitting with those memories after a particularly strong healing session, that I realised this was my rehearsal for my future career! I have always wanted to be in front of a crowd, talking, and spreading good vibes. The second time I revisited this, situation I started to understand that no matter how much I wish it was different, I am not going to be everyone's presenter of choice. You cannot please everyone. I am still working on integrating this lesson today, but I have started to feel proud of myself for being brave, getting up there and having a voice. I am understanding all of the experience, the good and the bad, and it helped me become who I am today.

Activity 9: Self-Healing

Find a space where you will not be disturbed. You can light some candles, burn some incense. Make the space feel special and sacred. Play your favourite gentle meditation music. Get a glass of water ready to drink at the end of the session. Either lie down or sit comfortably. Wrap yourself in a snuggly blanket if you feel the cold.

Follow your breath. Enjoy the simple rise and fall of your chest. Place your hands comfortably on your body. I like one hand over the centre of my chest and one on my tummy. Set your intention by asking for the healing energy to flow.

Feel your heart centre start to expand with the unconditional love of the Universe. Can you feel the flow of energy through your palms? Relax into the experience and let go. If you fall asleep, that is fine. It is what you need.

When you feel the energy flow start to stop, your healing is done! If at first you cannot feel it, just stop after fifteen minutes. In time, you will be able to experience physical sensations from healing and know when it has drawn to a close. Send out some thanks with a grateful heart to the Universe.

10
The Spirit Guides Frequency

We all have Spirit guides, a team of incredible teacher energies who gather around us for our own growth and development. They are with you right now. Some of your Spirit guides will have been with you from the moment you took your first breath and will be with you until you take your last. Some of your Spirit guides will have experienced other lives with you. Some of your Spirit guides will be with you just for this stage in your development, very much like teachers we have at school – here for the lessons you need to receive and gone when they are completed. Some of your Spirit guides you will call in through your own choice, inviting them in for what you want to learn.

Although we often perceive Spirit guides as individuals, I think we experience them that way for our own comfort. Spirit are part of that great oneness I mentioned earlier, but in our limited human consciousness it helps us to see them as an individual, just like we are. Often people I work with want to know what their Spirit guides look like and what form they take. This is such a fun way to work with Spirit. **However, the most important aspect of Spirit guides is the information they bring – their guidance, their wisdom.**

In our physical world, with our limited understandings, so much of our experience is absorbed through our physical senses. Our Spirit guides understand that, and they will never ever judge you for wanting to know what they look like. They hold a space of unconditional love for us unlike anything I have ever experienced on earth. That said, it always makes me sad when people who have been working with these incredible forces for many months can only share information about the clothes they are wearing, or the time period they come from. There is so much incredible untapped knowledge in those encounters.

I often find that people like to create a kind of Spirit guide hierarchy, almost like playing a game of Spirit Guide Top Trumps. They will say their Spirit guide is an archangel, not just an ordinary angel. Or they will claim their guide is a chieftain of some long lost Indigenous American tribe, or a Buddhist monk. What does it say about us and the valves we have turned on if we are not open to receiving a message from a Victorian chambermaid or an elderly woman who died in the 1970s? We set expectations for ourselves that Spirit needs to appear Spiritual. We turn away from an ordinary looking guide, hoping for something more exotic, more in keeping with our idea of Spirituality.

Look at yourself right now, as someone on the journey, as someone Spiritual. What are you wearing? I am wearing jeans, a t-shirt, a hoodie, and trainers. My hair needs a wash and I am not wearing any makeup. Does that make me more or less Spiritual? If I was presenting like this as a Spiritual guide, would you be open to receiving information from me?

How do our own judgements about what constitutes a Spiritual being hold us back from our own connections with Spirit? I am not saying you should ignore working with what your guide looks like. I am just recommending that in the beginning, do not fixate on appearances. Instead, build a relationship with your guides based on their teachings. The relationship is key here. Your objective is to build a strong and open friendship with your Spirit guides. The more you are comfortable and blended with them, the deeper your connection will be. The deeper the connection, the clearer the messages will be that you receive. The more you trust the messages (and your ability to hear them) the greater the understandings they can give you. Just like our relationships in this physical realm, the more effort and attention you spend on your Spirit guide family, the better that relationship will be.

Although the next activity will help you open up to Spirit guides, I want you to regard it as a casual, normal relationship. Start checking in with your guides when you are brushing your teeth, when you are cooking soup, or when you are on a dog walk. They are always with you and will always answer you. I find the best time to communicate with sprit guides is when I am doing repetitive boring tasks. My human brain is absorbed with the mundane and not getting in the way.

Spirit guides usually communicate with me in my own voice in my head. At first, I resisted thinking this is Spirit communicating with me. Is this the same voice that tells me I look fat in jeans? Is this the same voice that berates other drivers or slow supermarket walkers? Yes! This voice! The more I have learnt to trust and respond to that voice the greater my connection has become.

Activity 10: Spirit Guide Presence

Set your intention to work in the Spirit guide frequency by simply thinking, "I am working in the Spirit guide frequency." You can also visualise a line of switches, one for each frequency, and just flick the switch for the frequency you want to use. Settle your energy. Build your power. Hold that space for a moment. Become aware of the edge of your aura. Imagine it like a bubble of light that surrounds and permeates your physical self. Ask your Spirit guide to step forward.

Where do you feel like they have stepped forward from? Are they in front of you? Behind you? To the side? Do not get tangled up in worrying whether you are right or wrong. If you cannot feel it don't worry! Just ask them to come in where it feels comfortable to you. For example, you can say, "Spirit guide I can't feel you. Can you stand beside my left shoulder please?"

Allow that blending to take place. Imagine your energy merging with your Spirit guide's energy. Know that every breath you take allows that blend to go deeper and deeper. How does your Spirit guide feel to you? What emotions are you receiving from them? If you allow yourself to feel it, can you understand how much they love you? How proud of you they are? How happy they are to be connecting with you this way?

Communicate with them! If you are not feeling their presence, ask them to come closer. Remember you are in charge! If you do not like the experience or it feels like it is too much for, you can ask them to step back. They will do so, instantly.

Take your time with this. Do not push it too hard. Expect that you will doubt and disbelieve it, but Spirit are incredibly gentle. Just keep trying. Keep practising.

You can ask them to step back, too. Sometimes it is easier to feel them step out of your energy field, than step into it. You can ask Spirit to step in and out of your energy as many times as you like. When you feel like you have done enough (just a few minutes when you are first beginning) thank your guide and ask them to step back.

Take some long slow deep breaths. Focus on your physical self once more. Wiggle your fingers and toes. Stretch. Imagine that beautiful light you built up slowly fading until it is contained within you once more. Have a drink and stand up only when you feel ready.

When I first started working with Spirit guides like this, the emotional experience of receiving that unconditional love for them was too much for me. It was a running joke in my circle that "Hannah is crying again. Her guides must be here." I do not think as humans we ever experience true unconditional love. People have expectations and needs. Society has pressures and conformities. It was unlike anything I had ever experienced to just receive and be held in complete love with no requirement. I know that energy made me who I am today. Once I allowed myself to receive this unconditional love (and it is still a work in progress) it gave me the confidence to face my inner demons, to acknowledge the truth of who I really am, and the bravery to take the leap in my mediumship again and again!

Spirit bring nothing but unconditional love. If you are experiencing something other than that, it is your fear and lack of self-love clouding your connection – and that's okay. We all get in our own way sometimes! Acknowledge it and try to move past it to feel the purity of the Spirit connection. It may take several goes over time and that is okay too. Do not give in. Do not give up. Come back to it once a day over several days and see how it changes. As I said before, expecting a strong blend with Spirit on your first try is going to end in disappointment. But slowly, with concerted effort on your part, you will find that connection strengthens and builds.

Some of my Spirit guides have appeared soft and loving. Some have been more traditional teacher energies that were firm and definitive. Some have made me laugh until my sides hurt and others have been very serious and devout. All have brought nothing but love.

My own insecurities have sometimes clouded that connection. When I worked with my very first guide it was so nurturing, so filled with love, that I just floated in and was held for the entire session. When it was time for me to work with a new guide, they felt very different. I was a little intimidated and a bit scared, but then Spirit are not at all intimidating or scary! It was a different way of working that was uncertain to me, but it was also very important for my development. I needed to know things were changing and I needed to open up to the new experiences of it for my growth. Perceiving that guide are different helped me to do that.

Activity 11: Communicating with Purpose

Set your intention to work in the Spirit guide frequency. Use a simple thought or flick the switch! Settle your energy. Build your power. Hold that space for a moment.

Ask your Spirit guide to step forward. Where do you feel like they have stepped forward from? Are they in front of you? Behind you? To the side? Allow that blending to take place. Imagine your energy merging with your Spirit guide's energy. Know that every breath you take allows that blend to go deeper and deeper.

When you feel connected & ready ask them for an object. You may receive this as an image in your mind's eye, a word, a knowing etc. Do not push it! The answer is just there already. It's the first thing that popped in, regardless of whether it fits your idea of "Spiritual" or not. You are aiming to receive this information instantly. The longer you hold onto it the more you will begin to doubt it.

Now ask Spirit, "What does this object mean? What is the message?" Sometimes, when you have been given a particularly unexpected item, you will find your brain kicks in and your valves close. You think, "I can't possibly get a Spiritual message about a spanner!" This is a key journey that you need to undertake many times for mediumship development. Pushing through that voice again and again. Trust. I know, that is easier said than done.

Practice, practice, and practice some more. Remember the flow that you are aiming for in all mediumship – perceiving, receiving, allowing, and communicating. It might not happen instantly. It will not happen every time. But by doing this exercise on a regular basis, you are building up your ability to communicate with your Spirit guides on an ongoing basis.

When you feel like you have received the information (or that today is not your day) thank your guide and ask them to step back. Take some long slow deep breaths. Focus on your physical self once more. Wiggle your fingers and toes. Stretch. Imagine that beautiful light built up slowly fading until it is contained within you once more. Have a drink and stand up only when you feel ready.

In your notebook, write down the gift and message you received.

Spiritual Slaps

It is important to understand that Spirit guides do not take away the lessons we need to learn. It is my understanding that we are here to undergo certain physical experiences for our soul's development. For the most part, these lessons seem to centre around us forgetting our infinite power and potential, and being kicked around by ourselves, others, and life until we take control. I call these lessons Spiritual slaps, and they hurt! However, they are crucial for us discerning what is not working for us and leading us to making the changes we need.

When I took a shamanic course, I remember the teacher saying, "You have to learn to love your shit," when we were talking about our journeys and the difficulties we had faced along the way. I will admit that at the time, I was not buying into that at all! But I get it now. I am grateful for the lumps, bumps, and dumps I have had. Some I chose because I did not know better. Some I allowed because I did not believe I deserved better. Some I needed to open me up to the lesson, its teaching, and my unfoldment.

Your Spirit guides are not here to give you a map telling you which way to go. They do not stop the giant craters in the road appearing, seemingly out of nowhere. You are not here to experience a Spirit's life that is blissful peace and limitless potential. You are here to experience life as a human, including its lessons, learning, and growth. Spirit guides are here to open you up to your potential, to help you with creating the life you choose, and to support you when the shit hits the fan by helping you make better choices and pick up the pieces.

People often ask me in readings for clear answers about their future path. I always feel like I am disappointing them when I say the path is theirs to create. (I have to speak the truth as I perceive it.) We do not come here with a fully predestined path laid out. We choose that path as we walk it.

There may be experiences we agree to have before we come here, so yes, there are some aspects that are predestined. But not every step of our life is planned out ahead of time, to receive when it is time. Most of our existence here in the physical realm is subject to our choosing. And to be clear, we come here to choose. Therefore, Spirit will not choose for us.

What if the greatest lesson for your soul's growth is to experience the hardship of a relationship that damages you, crushes you until you hit rock bottom, and then to choose better for yourself? What if finding your inner strength to choose better is your reason for being here?

What if those people who came into your life who hurt you and made you feel small, where you bent yourself into the shape you felt would make them like you best, were doing you the biggest favour anyone will do for you in this lifetime?

What if your main objective in existing at this time is to find your voice and speak your truth, and while you are waiting for permission you are delaying your soul's purpose?

These lessons are necessary. They are why we are here. In the Spirit world there is nothing but joy, love, and happiness. There is no physical pain, no greed, no competition. There is an abundance of love, energy, and power.

I believe our purpose here is to experience what we need to, and then rise into an architect energy, where we understand we create this physical world by what we focus on, what we believe and what we choose.

So, then what is your guide's job? It is to inspire you to make better choices and learn from the lessons already experienced, to open you up to your potential and cheerlead you into a new life, and to commiserate and support you when you get in the way again.

Taking that further, it makes sense that sometimes our Spirit guides will invite experiences into our world that teach us what we need to know, even if they are not exactly comfortable! I think it is interesting to sit with this and really ponder. If a guide's job is to teach you, might they in fact encourage you to get into situations that maybe are not going to end well for the lesson you need to learn? I once went into business with a friend of mine. I knew it was a bad idea, but I kept hoping it would get better. It was a disaster. I just could not find my voice and kept allowing her to make decisions that didn't work for me. I went deeper and deeper down the rabbit hole. Finally, Spirit forced me to get myself out by giving me a situation I knew I could not come back from, and I had to extract myself from the business. It caused deep hurt and I lost my friend. This was a painful and upsetting time for both of us. She has never forgiven me.

I knew it was a bad idea and I knew it from the very start. But who chose this? Me! I did! Spirit did not appear as an effigy at the end of my bed, reading me a warning from a scroll, because they knew *I knew* it was a bad idea. I could feel it from the start, from the second I jumped in and agreed without thinking about it. That decision is on me. However, I am sure Spirit had a hand in it because it taught me so much. It was a great lesson for me from Spirit. I kept asking them to fix it, to take the problem away without me needing to face it, whilst still choosing it for myself and not saying anything. Burying my head in the sand of politeness, I had hoped it would go away.

I take much more time now when making decisions like this. I am more careful who I work with. I am clearer about what I want from the start. I am unafraid to say, "no," because I understand a "no" upfront is a thousand times easier than a "no" in six months' time. I enforce boundaries because I value my energy and attention. I speak up when it is not right for me. These lessons have been invaluable for me going forward. I am grateful for my shit!

Activity 12: Messages from Guides

You will need several sheets of paper, a pen or pencil, and half an hour. Set your intention to work in the Spirit guide frequency.

Write a question for your guides on the top of the paper. If you can't think of one you can ask one of these:

- How can I strengthen my connection to you?
- What should I focus on next for my journey?
- How can I take my healing to the next level?
- What is holding me back?
- Have you got any advice for me?)

Settle your energy. Build your power. Hold that space for a moment. Ask your Spirit guide to step forward.

Pick up your pen and start replying. At the beginning, it will feel like it's you replying. That is okay. Keep writing. As you write, surrender to the experience. Try to allow it to become a flow. Do not worry about spelling mistakes or punctuation. Write and write and write until you feel the energy start to dissipate and slow. When you are finished shake that poor, aching hand! Thank you guides for working with you.

Now read back what you have written. How does it feel? Do you feel like you wrote it all? Are they parts of it you do not remember writing? Are there paragraphs where the language is not quite like yours?

This is not a test where you get it 100% right the first time you do it (or the second, or the third time!). This is about allowing yourself to slowly become connected to Spirit and tapping into the wealth of knowledge and understanding they have. To begin with, it might feel like it's mostly written from you, but the more you do this, the more that connection will grow and the more Spirit will be able to say through you. Who knows? One day you might find yourself collaborating with Spirit, writing a book as a guide to help others on their journey!

As I mentioned earlier, there are more than just Spirit guides who work with us for our growth and development. There are also angels, archangels, ascended masters, and ancestors. I still tune into the Spirit guide frequency to work with them, but I specify who I would like to communicate with. Sometimes one of them will appear without me expecting or seeking it. I experience them all very differently from each other and I find the information they bring differs, too. It is great practice to expand into and experience lots of different energies over time. There are some activities in this book in the "Taking it Further" section to help inspire you, but this next activity is the way I started working with my guardian angel.

Your guardian angel is an angel who has chosen to work with you in this lifetime, and potentially many other lifetimes, too! They bring that clarity and connection from the angelic realm, but also messages that are specific and pertinent to you and your journey. You can build a relationship and deep, meaningful connection with this being and lean on them as often as you wish to, for them to bring their guidance, support and unconditional love to you. You may have more that one guardian angel, so be open to experiencing different energies from different beings and play in that wonderful energy!

Activity 13: Working with my Guardian Angel

Set your intention to work in the Spirit guide frequency. Settle your energy. Build your power. Hold that space for a moment. Ask your angel guide to step forward. If you have been practising with Spirit guides for some time the energy of your angel might feel very different to you, in my understanding they come from a higher frequency plane and so it has more of an impact on our energy when we experience them! Allow that blending to take place. Imagine your energy merging with your angel guide's energy. Know that every breath you take allows that blend to go deeper and deeper.

How does your angel guide feel to you? Imagine them wrapping you up in their love. Feel their comforting presence. Realise how loved you are and visualise that energy being absorbed into every molecule of your being. Feel that love flowing through you, overcoming your barriers, clearing your energy. Relax into receiving that love. Drift off in that love.

When it is time, you will slowly start to become aware of your physical self once more. This could be a couple of minutes or half an hour! Your angel knows exactly what you need to receive. As you come back ask your angel for their name. It will be the first one that pops into your head. Do not push for it. If you do not get it this time you can try again next time.

Take some long slow deep breaths. Focus on your physical self once more. Wiggle your fingers and toes. Stretch. Take some time to allow yourself to become fully present with your physical self once more. You will have travelled further than you realise.

Once you have their name, you can start calling them in using their name specifically if you wish. Although Spirit do not hold the same value as we do on names and labels, it makes it a more personal relationship for us in our human experience, and helps us to accept their energy, wisdom, and love.

II
The Evidential Mediumship Frequency

Evidential mediumship seems to be the aspect that makes most developing mediums panic, but it's my favourite thing in the whole world! When you are connecting in the evidential mediumship frequency, you are perceiving and receiving factual information from the Spirit communicator to be able to prove their existence to your sitter (the person the reading is for). Evidential mediumship is about so much more than getting a checklist of information from the Spirit world and using it to prove who you are communicating with. Evidential mediumship is about reuniting someone in the physical realm with their much-loved friend or family member who has returned to the nonphysical.

I think for many mediums, the black and white nature of evidential mediumship can hold them back because it can lead to a fear of getting it wrong. Think of it this way: If you gave someone a message from Spirit guides that says "You will have twists and turns in the path ahead but it's taking you to where you need to be," that is a message that can apply to most people. But if you have an evidential connection with a mother who smoked a pipe, that is going to be objectively either right or wrong. This is where we mediums can get our knickers in a twist!

So many people hold themselves back from this sacred, transformational work because they do not feel good enough. Do not let that happen to you! You need to view it like this: If you were to move into the Spirit world tomorrow, you would watch your family from the non-physical realm carrying on with their life, missing you, talking about you, and wishing you were there for all the big life events. And you would be with them! If you are lucky, you might even be "felt" or acknowledged on occasion. Then imagine your beloved family member goes to see a medium. You can't wait for the chance to prove that you are there, that you are okay, that you are watching, and are still a part of their life. Would you judge that medium, working out if they were good enough, or calculating their hours of practice? Wouldn't you step forward if you knew it could be wonderfully healing for your relative to hear from you? You would take any and every opportunity! I know I would. The experience could also benefit the medium in their learning, too! It is a "win-win" situation. Spirit are already with you. You just have to open up and receive.

Evidential mediumship is usually carried out on a one-on-one reading basis, or in front of an audience (known as platform mediumship). When you work one-on-one, there is no doubt who the communicator is for. You normally have a longer session and can go deeper with the information. When you work on platform, you need to work more quickly as the audience are all hoping for a message. You need to find the correct recipient and bring through enough evidence to convince the recipient you are communicating with their loved one.

What Makes Good Evidential Mediumship?

There are so many different types of evidential mediumship, and most mediums work differently. Some of this is to do with which of our valves are open and it also tailored by our personal preferences. When I first started working with Spirit, we were given a list of items to receive from the communicator. It was a mental checklist that was ticked off as you received each thing. As I have developed and worked on my connection, I learnt to move past that approach, and Spirit now have me working in a very different way.

I have watched hundreds of other mediums work. I have done thousands of evidential communications myself. In my opinion (and it is only my opinion and personal preference) good mediumship is when you <u>feel</u> the presence of the communicator – it is when the sitter feels like they are reunited with their loved one again, or when an audience is moved by the presence of the Spirit world, even if the communication is not for them.

Good mediumship is watching a medium work with integrity and trust, convinced of their ability to communicate with the other side, and working with so many valves open, they are able to receive unique evidence.

I like my mediumship to show the personality of the Spirit I am communicating with. It has been amazing for me to witness how the essence of us remains the same in Spirit. We lose toxic traits or behaviours, but keep our spark, our personality, and our sense of humour. Whether they are righting wrongs, thanking the sitter for the help they gave them, remembering happier times together, or showing that they have been around for the moments in the sitter's life since they passed, these beautiful moments with Spirit are what makes it magical for me.

The wonderful thing is, the readings are always evidential, but they are not limited by the list of items I was trained to receive.

Good mediumship is surrendering and having trust that the Spirit will take us where they need to for the best possible outcome for all.

Service

Mediumship is about being in service to both the Spirit world and the people in front of you. It is about finding a place where you can satisfy the needs of both and trying as hard as you can to allow that to happen, without letting your doubt and expectation get in the way! You must also remember to be in service to yourself, too. So many forget this. Mediumship costs a lot in energy, and to be the best medium you need to be in a good physical state. Do not allow yourself to burn out, or for your needs to become secondary to your mediumship. You are a Spirit, too!

The Process

You start with intention, not because I believe the Spirit world require our instruction, but because it helps prepare your energy. By now you have been working on clearing as much of your blackboard as you can. You have been practising getting into your power often. You have been receiving communications from Spirit guides and learning to blend. Set your intention to work with the evidential mediumship frequency. Now, you just ask a Spirit communicator to step forward.

If you were reading for someone else, in your mind you would state, "I would like to work with a Spirit communicator for [sitter's name]." When I am working on the platform, I ask, "for Spirit communicators that can be easily understood by the audience, that will help build the energy I need to work."

You want to be in a space where you are just receiving the information, with as many valves open as possible, and the evidence flowing in. Avoid trying to "seek" the evidence, because as soon as you do that, you are closing valves and making it very hard for Spirit to work. You want to bring yourself into a state of surrender to offer the best from your mediumship, allowing Spirit to take control and chose the evidence, resulting in better connections. This is harder than it sounds, especially at the beginning of your development.

Switching Frequencies

When we are <u>seeking</u> information, we are working in a psychic frequency. When we are <u>receiving</u> information, we are working in an evidential mediumship frequency. In my opinion, the process for evidential mediumship has stages, and even though we want to work in the evidential mediumship frequency, we find ourselves starting in the psychic frequency.

In the initial moments as the Spirit communicator steps forward, you are seeking some validation that there is a Spirit there and that you are getting it right. Your imposter syndrome is in full force and you thinking you cannot do this. (By the way, this feeling will never change. I still have my evil twin piping up in demonstrations and readings, telling me I cannot do it. Fortunately, I have done enough work on myself and have had enough practice that I am able to ignore her and carry on regardless. Sadly, there is no shortcut. It comes with time and endurance.) You think there is a Spirit there, but is it? You think it's a man. Is that right? He feels like a dad, but are you making that up? At this stage, you are <u>psychically</u> reading a Spirit that has stepped forward to work with you, and that is okay. Because you set your intention to work in the evidential mediumship frequency, you will find yourself gently switching into it as the reading progresses.

Spirit Communication

It is important to remember that Spirit are energy. They are no longer in a physical, human body. When I used to watch *Ghost Whisperer* and *Medium* on the television, I would see the actors talking to Spirit like I talk to you. I have never met a medium for whom this is the case, although I am still looking! Spirit no longer have a voice box like they did when they were in human form. That is why we communicate with them through devices like Spirit boxes and Ouija boards. When you are working an evidential connection, you are receiving information in the form of energy, through those clair senses we talked about earlier. It is playing that game of energy charades!

It would be wonderful if we could just hear Spirit's voice. There would be no doubt, would there? You could tune in, give a name, address, date of birth, and a message, and move on to the next person. A whole audience could be read for in one night! But that is not how it works. The Spirit world are sending you information that you are perceiving through your valves and your clair senses. They know the best evidence to send

- Through which of your valves are open,
- Through your experiences and understandings,
- Which will make most sense to the sitter,
- Which will help the sitter know who they are, and
- Which will fulfil the greatest need.

This is the hard thing about evidential mediumship. Sometimes sitters arrive with their own list of evidence they expect to receive and are disappointed when you do not get it exactly right for them. But you are limited by what you are able to receive, and it varies from moment to moment. I have had sitters arrive asking for a password that they set with their loved one on their death bed. That would be easy and understandable to receive if they spoke to me, but we are dealing with energy!

I once had an audience member at a live event show me that no matter how hard you try, you cannot always satisfy the needs of a sitter. After providing fifteen pieces of evidence, including how they died, how long ago they died, their job, their personality, and their relationship, I was still hitting a wall with her. She begrudgingly gave me yesses that sounded like nos. When I asked, "Are you understanding all this because I'm not feeling like I'm getting the reaction I'd expect?" she folded her arms across her chest and said, "Tell me his name and I'll tell you if you're with me." This is the irony – in seeking a name you change the frequency to psychic and are then less likely to receive a name. Mediumship is all about surrender and trust. If I get a name, I always give it, but I trust Spirit know when they are able to get that information through me, and when it's better to go with something else.

It is even harder dealing with your own expectations of what you think you should be able to achieve. It is important to avoid being the thief of your own joy. Do not always look for what you could have done better, or what you think wasn't good enough. Instead, celebrate the wins and be open and optimistic about future growth.

Momentum

I am obsessed with momentum building in mediumship. It is the best way to get the most out of your evidential communication.

Think of your reading like an old steam train. You are the new driver on your first day at work. You start by looking at the track ahead. It is going up a mountain road and you are at the bottom. It feels overwhelming and impossible. You see other drivers with other trains making the journey and setting off, flying off up that track, but you have no idea how to make that happen for you.

First of all, just start! If you do not put any coal into the furnace, you are never going to get moving. Open up to Spirit and give what you get – and give it quickly. Just like stoking an engine, you do not want to be slowly investigating each piece of coal, studying it, and holding on to it. You need to chuck it on that fire and get this thing roaring. It is the same with mediumship. Do not make it slow. Do not hold onto the evidence to double check whether you are right. Just give it. Each piece of evidence is a scoop of coal on your furnace. As you keep delivering item after item as quickly as you can, the connection with the Spirit will start to build and build and build. Without realising, it you will become aware that your train has left the station! After you perfect the art of getting that momentum built, and realise the train is running along the tracks and making good headway, you can relax into the communication and get deeper, clearer evidence.

I see so many mediums become almost hypnotised by the first few pieces of evidence they receive. The problem with this is they have not built enough momentum yet to stop building the fire. The power ebbs, the blending slows down, and before you know it they are struggling to maintain their connection. Their self-doubt is now driving their train. They are leaning back on the shovel, talking all about how they knew they couldn't do it anyway.

I find that focusing on building that energy at the beginning sets you up for the rest of the reading. Also, the quicker you deliver the evidence, the less chance there is for you to get in the way!

You Are An Infection!

I know, that is not the nicest image to give you here, but it works! Imagine your brain holds a highly contagious virus. It is flowing through your whole body, but as the host, it doesn't impact you. It impacts your interpretation from Spirit.

<u>The key to evidential mediumship is to say what you get.</u> This frequency is not about you *interpreting* anything you receive. Spirit are delivering it to you in its entirety. The longer you hold onto a piece of evidence, double checking it, analysing it, trying to make sense of it, the more you infect it with the virus of you.

If you see an apple, you say, "Apple!" You do not say, "I am seeing an apple, and this means you maybe need to eat more fruit," or "I am thinking an apple for teacher so maybe you should be teaching now," or "I think this Spirit liked to eat apples." Just say, "Apple," and if the energy built allows, invite Spirit to explain why they have shown it to you. What is the feeling, the story, or the memory? Do not get caught up trying to work that out for yourself. It must come from the communicator, not you!

It Is Not About You!

Gosh, I know it feels like it is about you. When someone is in front of you and you are trying to please them, trying to fulfil a need and simultaneously deal with the choking fear rising within you, it sure does feel like it is all about you, but it isn't! As soon as you hold on to a piece of evidence and start trying to interpret it, you are infecting it with you. That virus has started shifting it, changing it, making it less pure and unrecognisable from what it started out as. You are the translator. And just like a translator, you are not supposed to edit, change, or make sense of what you are getting. Just simply say it. It is not for you. It is for your sitter. Deliver it quickly, as soon as you get it. Get it away from your virus (your thoughts). Your understanding and your mediumship will thank you for it!

Do Not Be Hypnotised By What You See

For most people who start working with Spirit, they are building their own language and understanding of their own mediumship. I often find that we use the resource of our own minds and knowledge base when communicating. You know that blend I mentioned to you earlier? At the beginning of a reading, you can expect it to look like 10% Spirit and 90% you. This means Spirit are mostly using what you know and what you have experienced to provide the evidence.

For example, when I first started working with Spirit, if it was a grandfather, I would see an image in my mind's eye of my own grandfather. I panicked, not trusting the intelligence of the Spirit world, and I would ask him to step back so I could work with my sitter's relatives. Eventually I realised it was not my grandfather. Rather, it was merely my brain interpreting the Spirit and using the closest reference point it could. Thus, a grandfather became <u>my</u> grandfather. As I have progressed, I do not even see images now. I just *know* the relationship. It does get easier with time!

What can happen at the beginning is that students see an image in their mind's eye and believe it to be fact. This can lead to a lot of "no's" that don't need to be "no's"! I remember reading for someone at the beginning of my journey with Spirit and it went something like this:

> Me: I'm seeing a toy duck.
>
> Sitter: Yes, oh my goodness!
>
> Me: (Getting full on hypnotised with the image in my mind, which was actually a toy duck from a book my sister had when we were little.) It's yellow and fluffy and has a blue bow around its neck.
>
> Sitter: No, it was not like that at all. (Disappointment and doubt are written all over their face.)

What happened there was I had not blended fully with the Spirit. I had not built enough momentum to take the reading forward. I drew the flow of energy to a halt by stopping to investigate the image in my mind. The image that was actually drawn from my own imagination, and not from the Spirit world. The *energy* of toy duck came from the Spirit world and my brain had made it into an image. Do you see the difference?

I always suggest that you start a reading by quickly progressing through the surface level of what you receive, following the knowing and feeling clairs. Don't delve too deeply into anything you "see" or "hear" until your momentum is fully built and your blending with Spirit is well underway. You can get so much information that is still very evidential this way. As you blend more with Spirit they will bring back any evidence from earlier in the reading that has space for expansion and deeper meaning when the time is right.

Starting Off Psychic

As I mentioned above, we often start off seeking in the psychic frequency, even when we want to be working with the evidential mediumship frequency. As we get used to the experience and the frequency of the Spirit we have to allow ourselves to expand into our power. When we are receiving, we are getting what the Spirit world know is best to send us. When we are seeking, we are just getting what we have picked up on first.

Think about your life and the relationships you have in it. Your parents have experienced a different version of you to your partner, your children, your friends, and your colleagues. When Spirit are sending the information for us to receive, they tailor it to the needs of the sitter. They show the version of them that makes the most sense to the person who has come for the reading.

I find that the things we feel from a Spirit remain generally more constant than what we see or hear. My grandmother is a great example of this. When mediums *feel* into her soul, they feel how dynamic she was, her independence, her fun-loving side, that she liked to talk, and her confidence. This is all correct. When mediums try to *see* her they always see her as younger than she was when she passed. This is technically incorrect and would result in a "no" from most sitters. It was very confusing at the beginning when people would mention a woman with black hair who passed in her 50s. It makes so much sense with my Nanna's personality. She was very proud of how she looked when she was younger and was always very glamourous, so I understand why that would be the strongest thing someone sees when they connect with her psychically.

Activity 14: How Do Others See Us?

A slightly macabre but good, fun exercise is to sit with members of your family and everyone to write down four things they would expect to see as evidence if you were in Spirit. This could include memories of special moments, personality traits, appearance, objects with significance, facts about you etc. You may well be surprised with what people bring up! How many of you have picked the same things to describe you? When we did it in my family hardly any of us had the same things. They were all true but were important to us from *our* point of view. As humans we all experience things differently, even the same things!

This is the amazing power of Spirit. They know what the sitter understands to be valid and work within the confines of what you are able to receive as a medium.

Structure for a One-on-One Reading

Once you are comfortable with holding your power and feeling more confident with your abilities, this structure will naturally change, but this is the way I teach all my students to work to begin with.

I want you to think of some bite size bits of evidence you would like to receive from your communicator, either things you can easily feel or just know. My suggestions are things such as:

- Relationship (e.g., parent, grandparent, friend, colleague, child etc)
- Type of relationship (e.g., close, distant, troubled, loving)
- Personality of the Spirit
- Things that Spirit enjoyed when they were in human form
- Connected relationships of the Spirit (e.g., I have your grandmother here, and she makes me aware of your grandfather with her.)
- Age at passing (e.g., child, teenager, young adult, 30s-50s, middle-aged, 60s-70s, but not trying to get a specific number)
- How you feel they passed
- Whether passing was over a longer period or sudden
- How long ago they passed
- Their job, work, passions, or hobbies

Feel free to add to this or use what you are drawn to.

Being aware of the potential items Spirit can bring to your attention when you are building momentum helps to open your valves and make it easier. This is not about pushing into a seeking energy. This is about relaxing into a receiving energy. If you have some idea of what you are likely to receive, you can surrender into that to start the reading off. Do not get fixated on the order or getting everything on that list. Just being aware of what you could receive will help.

Keep that focus on being quick. Remember the virus! Get it out of you before you infect it. Once you have a few bullet points ticked off, and hopefully your sitter is recognising who you are communicating with and giving you feedback as you go, you will feel a point where Spirit take over. It may take quite some time and practice to experience this. It took me a couple of years! Do not get disheartened. This is about learning to surrender and it is the hardest thing to do! We are trained to think intellectually from birth and disassociate from our knowing and feeling sense. Mediumship is about undoing all of that.

Regardless of whether you feel it or not, once you've got the momentum built, move as much as possible into the space of surrender. Let Spirit take control. Spirit will take into account the sitter's need, expectation, and the relevance. Now it is up to the Spirit to show you what they want to. You can expect this evidence to go deeper, to have more detail, and be more specific. Rather than moving on to the next piece of evidence as quickly as you can, allow space for it to expand. Feel into it. Do you feel like there is more?

It will work like this:

1. I am seeing a pocket watch (seeing)
2. The pocket watch is very ornate, with an intricate lid (seeing)

3. I know your grandfather wore this watch and used it often (knowing)
4. Your grandfather was very precise with time and liked to have his routine kept the same (feeling)
5. He liked his meat and two veg and had his dinner at the same time every day (tasting/smelling, hearing)
6. This watch was very precious and belonged to his father (feeling)
7. The watch has been passed on to a male in your family (feeling, knowing, hearing)

Your evidence is like building blocks. You will not get the information for the second block until you have spoken aloud the information from the first block. You need the first block spoken and acknowledged before you get the next one. You will be receiving the information about the second block as you state the details from the first. Your aim here is to allow the connection and evidence to go deeper and clearer, whilst not pausing and maintaining the momentum. You want a flow. Remember that steam train! Holding onto information, trying to get clarity or double check what you already know stops that flow. The more you are in the flow the easier the reading is, you are less in the way when the blend is strong. It does not always work like that, we often get in our own way and stop the flow, lose momentum. When that happens, you need to go back to bullet pointing evidence with speed and build that momentum once more.

When you feel like you have given enough evidence you can then move to message. I find this element has a different frequency and is perfect for starting to allow everything to slow down and become gentle. Your train is over the top of the mountain now, and the rest is a smooth slow journey into the station.

Activity 15: Practice Spirits

Did you know that the Spirit world is full of wonderful people who would love to come and help you with your development? The best way to learn to communicate with Spirit is to practice with the Spirit world!

Set your intention to work with the evidential mediumship frequency. Ask to work with a Spirit who can teach you with what you need to experience at this time. Power up and clear your mind. Allow yourself a maximum of three slow breaths for this. You have been practising so much now, you are adept enough at it! Feel that Spirit stood beside you. Can you feel their gender? Can you feel the relationship? Can you feel their personality? Thank them for the connection and let them step back.

Write down your findings in your notebook. If you feel that you are able, have another go! Go back into your power and start the process again with another Spirit. Keep practising again and again. None of these Spirits will be connected to you, or anyone you know. This is purely about opening up your valves, and you starting to understand how your mediumship works.

You can also use the activity for specific evidence points you want to expand on. For example, when I wanted to work on getting better, clearer evidence on passings, I would ask the Spirit world to work with me this way so I could feel into different experiences of death and feel different illnesses in my physical body.

Getting Feedback

There reaches a point in every developing medium's journey where they plateau. This plateau is because there is a limit to how far we can develop our evidential mediumship alone. It is time to work with others! I find that most developing mediums hold themselves back at this point. They think, "I am not ready," or "I don't feel confident!" You will <u>never</u> feel ready or confident! If mediumship is calling you, and you want to do it, that is enough. You will never get to the standard of being good enough to read for other people without the experience of reading for other people. Oh, the irony!

You will have found doing the exercise above is equally mind blowing. But you will also be doubting what you are receiving and thinking you could be making it up. The only way you will know if you are communicating with Spirit is to work with someone unconnected to you, bring someone in, and get evidence they can verify. This is also a very important part of the energetic experience of mediumship. We need the energy of a sitter to build the momentum to get up the mediumship mountain!

The simple truth is you will never do a reading in the full power of the Spirit world without a sitter. The sitter brings the source of what needs to be fulfilled. That need has its own energy and is a charge that powers the reading.

So, whether you have zero experience and found this book by accident, or you have been waiting in the wings for Spirit to call for you, you need to take the leap and push yourself into a practice scenario.

Here is some of the ways you can practice:

- Find a local circle/mediumship group if there is one near you. My first circle was a 90-minute round trip for me, but I still went every week. I know some people who have studied in circles and had amazing experiences and others who have not. The most important thing is that it feels like the right space for you. Do not settle. I know people who have had their confidence damaged by settling for the wrong group for them.
- Find an online practice group. Again, there is a huge number when you search for them. Do not be afraid to experiment.
- Invite willing friends over and practice on them. Make sure you are clear that you are learning and just starting out. Work with friends who make you feel safe and comfortable.
- Join a group or a course either online or in person. Often, I found this to be the best option. People committing to pay brings a more dedicated set of students, and you will have a teacher on hand to guide you!

You need feedback. You need to know what you are getting right and where you need to work. Feedback is a double-edged sword. Tt shows you that you are actually doing this! Amazing! But it also shows you what you are getting wrong, which is always an uncomfortable experience.

One of the biggest lessons I had to learn was that not everyone who is in a Spiritual group behaves with integrity. We are all humans, and in honesty, some of the hardest sitters I have had have been developing mediums. This can be for a variety of reasons. Sometimes they are nervous themselves and mistakenly believe if you don't do well, it will make them look better. Sometimes they are so busy interpreting it for you that they forget to listen and receive. Sometimes they are limited by the teaching they have had before. I have heard some classics in my time, including a friend of mine who was told that she couldn't possibly have had a Spirit connection in a such a short time (she was on her second course), and was making it up!

The Mediumship Triangle

I view the mediumship reading energy like the fire triangle, but instead of fuel, air, and heat, it looks like this:

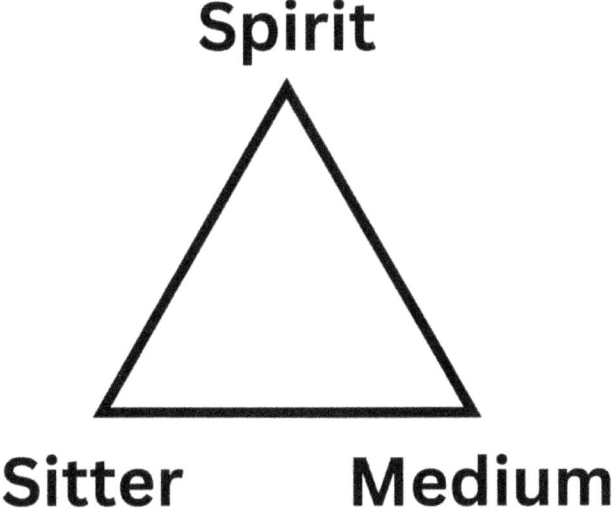

You need all three elements to create a great reading.

Spirit are always in perfect alignment and will do whatever they can to make the reading work. Your own energy can often pull a reading out of a good energetic space. Are your nerves getting the better of you? Are you tired, overwhelmed, stressed, or doubting your abilities? Part of your development is learning how to draw a sitter's energy into a reading. Your bullet-pointed evidence should help with that process. Every "yes" you get will pull their energy into the mix. This is why you see demonstrating mediums on the platform asking the recipient to use their voice in responding. It completes that energetic triangle.

Use your psychic abilities at the start of a reading to find out how to deliver the reading, and tailor it to your sitter. Do they need it soft, gentle, slow, and steady? Are they all business and want it quick and decisively? It is vital to understand that no matter how hard you try, some sitters are difficult. They may not understand how mediumship works, have unrealistic expectations, or be there purely to test you. If you get a sitter like this, do not let it ruin your confidence. Be strong and tell them you do not think you have a compatible energy and suggest they find another medium. If you do decide to go ahead, know that without their energy bringing good vibes into the reading, there is a limit to how deeply you can blend and access evidence.

Getting Comfortable With "No's"

When I first started mediumship, I thought the aim was to get it right all of the time. Having grown up on a diet of heavily edited television shows about mediumship, I believed that if I practised and worked hard I would get to a point where the only response I received was, "Yes". The Spirit world have shown me abundantly how very wrong I was!

Firstly, you are a human being. There will be moments where you misinterpret, misunderstand, or even just make stuff up! That is natural and to be expected. Your work here is to accept that, and not let it pull you out of your power. Secondly, your sitter is a human being too. Having a reading is a pressured experience. They are trying to remember all these different things about their loved one, waiting for their expectation to be fulfilled, whilst having an emotional reaction to being back in contact with them. It is a lot for one person to process. Expectations can hold you back. Most sitters come with a mental list of expectations that they want you to fulfil. If they are expecting you to talk about their mum's divorce and you are talking about the ring she left behind, you will find you often get "no's" that are not really "no's". It is a right of passage to learn how to hold your power and making sure your sitter is answering correctly! It is very hard at the beginning of a reading when you are trying to build that momentum and you hear "no". More often than not this is due to the sitter wanting to hear from someone specific, and someone else steps forward. Imagine you have gone for a reading to hear from your son, but your grandmother is stepping forward. You would be understandably disappointed, but it does not mean that the medium is wrong. The Spirit world know who the best contact is to bring forward at this time, for both you as the medium and for the sitter who is on their healing journey.

When I started working the platform it used to frustrate me when I would get a Spirit for whom no one would put their hand up. Having done so many audience readings I have learnt to have more compassion. People often contact me after events to say it was for them but they were too upset and shocked to put their hand up. Usually everything I said was correct too! This is the perfect example of how mediumship keeps you humble. I would love to look amazing in front of the audience every night, but it is not about me, is it? I am still fulfilling the need for that Spirit and that recipient.

Sometimes in the pressure of the moment a sitter might forget a piece of evidence. Sometimes they might not know. You have to trust that Spirit know what they are doing. There will be a reason why that particular piece of evidence was presented for that particular sitter.

I want to tell you a story here, which I hope will help you to understand how Spiritual teaching works. When I started feeling drawn to platform/audience readings I had quite a learning curve. I now love being on a stage with an audience. I now love the feeling of it, the buzz, the atmosphere. When I first wanted to practice platform, I used to host small events in my home for friends and people I knew locally. I'd have 12-15 people crammed into my reiki studio. Because everyone had come out for the night, I had no choice but to work for an hour to an hour and a half to make it worth their while. I would have loved a group to learn in where I could have done one contact and sat back down whilst someone else worked, but that was not my path.

I was *so* petrified of hearing "no's" If I got a "no", I would freak out. No one would know externally, but internally my inner demons would take control, reminding me I wasn't any good and that I shouldn't be doing this. My vibration would plummet instantly as soon as I heard a "no". This would stop my blend, interrupt my flow, and slow my momentum, thereby lowering the standard of my evidence.

When I was connecting to my Spirit guides for advice they kept warning me that I needed to get comfortable with "no's". I kept interpreting this as "the no's will go". And, of course, they did not, as this was not what Spirit meant. You cannot expect to have no "no's" when there are so many variables, and most of them are out of your control.

Spirit kept telling me to get confident with "no's". I kept hoping the "no's" would go. Eventually, Spirit decided action must be taken! How did I get over my fear of "no's"? By the biggest Spiritual slap of my journey so far. A night of nothing but "no's"! Not one piece of evidence was taken. Not one Spirit was recognised. I had an audience of sympathetic but embarrassed faces staring at me. It was 90 minutes of pain.

I quit mediumship. Sobbing into a Toblerone I swore I would never work as a medium again. I was done. Forever. This was also the greatest gift Spirit ever gave me, because even though I was devastated, I could not walk away from mediumship. I was obsessed with it. It was my calling. It just kept calling me. And when I went back, I was not afraid of "no's" anymore. I had experienced my worst case scenario. It had happened. My worst fear had become my reality and I had survived. It was not comfortable. It was not pretty. I cried for three days, but I still went back and now I knew it would not stop me.

There Is No Such Thing As A Perfect Reading

There is always regret with a reading. There was something you missed. There was something you misinterpreted or could have done better. There was a moment where you got in the way. There was a lack of surrender.

Mediumship is always a work in progress. Some readings are better than others. Mostly for me, that is determined by how I feel I did, whether I have that experience of Spirit taking the wheel, or whether I feel that I was too in control. No matter how you feel you did, there is always learning, as there should be! I do not ever want to stop being amazed by Spirit. As long as you tried, you did enough. It is pretty miraculous when you think about it. You are communicating with the Spirit world. Amazing!

12
The Trance Frequency

Trance is the deepest blend with Spirit where, to a certain extent, you allow such a deep connection with them that they can use your physical body to speak or become a conduit for healing. Some mediums believe that trance is where you should start your journey, and other believe you need to be established in your connection. I have included this frequency as the final one, because I feel you should be confident in the security of your work with Spirit. By this I do not mean you need to be more developed or ascended to a specialist frequency. The work in trance will create that as you go along, but I do believe you should feel safe and comfortable. Trance will shift your energy and align your vibration the more you work with it. Trance simply will not work if you are scared of it! Fear will create resistance which will stop the experience. You cannot surrender your physical self to something you are uncertain of. This is an exercise in trust. So, take a moment to really assess how you feel about your relationship with the Spirit world before you even attempt trance.

Now although I have listed trance as a separate frequency, it really covers both the Spirit guide, evidential, and healing frequencies, but in a much deeper way:

- You can use trance with your Spirit guide for them to speak advice, guidance, and inspiration through your body using your voice box.
- You can blend with someone's loved one in Spirit to allow them to speak through you.

- You can work in the trance frequency to become a conduit for deep, meaningful healing.

Many mediums say that trance is a complete surrender of our physical selves. I do not. I believe this is a deep blend (the deepest blend available) but we are still a little bit present. If we work on the basis that a fantastic blend for evidential mediumship is 80%, then trance would be more like 90%. I have searched and searched to find a trance medium with a 100% blend. To me, they would be able to speak in a language they are unaware of, or who could become my grandmother and give me irrefutable evidence that they are not only communicating with her, but actually *are* her. (Surely, if my Nan was speaking there would be no mistakes and the evidence would be all clear, specific and correct). I am yet to find anyone. This is not a failing, though. I find it empowering. This just shows how all mediumship is truly a collaboration with Spirit. It is working *with* us, not instead of us.

It is important to be realistic with your approach to trance. It is a deep blend and a deep surrender, but it is not your consciousness exiting stage left while another Spirit takes control of your physical body. Trance is a brilliant energy to sit in to strengthen your blend in other frequencies of your mediumship. The more you get accomplished at blending and surrendering in trance, the more you can do it in the Spirit guide and evidential frequencies.

To work in trance, you simply set your intention to be in that frequency. Tune in your mental radio, flick that switch, or simply ask.

Trance unfoldment is a lengthy process. You will need to be dedicated and willing to sit in the energy several times a week over several months with the expectation of potentially not experiencing anything. It takes many adjustments to our energy bodies and time away from the experience to integrate the adjustments. You need to be in it for the long haul!

Find yourself a quiet space where you will not be disturbed. If you wish, you can play some gentle music to cover any background noise. Sudden noises in your home will bring you out of the experience very easily. Allow yourself to settle your energy. I recommend starting with guides. I have not yet mastered a complete reading with loved ones in Spirit. I think it helps the process to work with the same Spirit over time and build that trust, familiarity, and relationship.

Set your intention to work in trance. You may immediately feel a difference in the energy that surrounds you. Imagine your trance guide stepping closely beside you. Take a moment to be present with that feeling. Ask them to step nearer. Take a moment to surrender to that feeling. Ask them to come nearer. Pause and surrender. Blend. Pause and surrender. Blend deeper. Pause and surrender. Blend deeper.

Imagine your soul making way in your physical body for the guide. Sometimes I fold myself up like a piece of origami. Other times I visualise stepping back and making space. Allow Spirit to fill that space. Relax into it. Like all work with Spirit, you will find moments where the blend feels incredible and strong and other moments where you are back in your head. That is okay! Any time you realise you are back, just allow yourself to gently move back into the trance energy.

You may feel different physical sensations. Your throat may start to feel dry or tickly, like there is a lump in it. Your heart may start to beat differently. Your breathing rate might change. There may be tingling sensations or heat. You are in control. If something makes you uncomfortable, ask Spirit to stop. Explain your needs and experience to the Spirit you are working with. A thought, as always, is enough. (e.g., "I'm not feeling anything," or "I don't like the sensation in my throat.")

Allow yourself to gently build into trance. Start with sitting in the energy for just five minutes. Over time, as you develop your confidence and ability to sit in trance energy, increase the time slowly. Once you are adept at holding the power you can decide how you want to use it. Intention is all. For example:

- To work with healing, just ask for that flow to begin and practice becoming the conduit for the energy. Your hands may gently begin to move as you experience the fullness of the blend. Let Spirit lead you.
- To work with speaking, set that intention. Allow the blend to build in your voice box. As Spirit take greater control of your physical self, your mouth may start to move. You may feel your tongue move too. Start with just making a sound. Then aim for one word, then a sentence, and so on! At the beginning you may find just making a sound pulls you out of your power. Keep practising and growing in belief and confidence.

In the beginning, you will find that the time you experience in trance is very short. Once you are able to hold that connection for longer, you can record yourself to hear the words that Spirit speak through you. Although your voice may change in tone and inflection, it will still be your voice coming out of your body. My trance guide, Charles, is much posher than me and speaks in a very different way, but he is still using my voice box!

Coming back from trance takes time. When Spirit step back, allow yourself a long time to reconnect with your physical self. Loud noises and negative vibrational energies (such as turning on the television to watch the news) can have a greater impact from the heightened frequency of trance, because there is just too much contrast. Allow time to be present with the physical realm once more, gently, and slowly. Have a big drink of water. Take it slow. If you feel a bit disconnected or dizzy, go for a barefoot walk in the garden or imagine roots growing out of your feet into the Earth. Walking in nature is good, too. Reconnect with the physical space.

Even the slightest blend with trance energy can have amazing transformational benefits. I find students become more trusting in what they are receiving during readings. Their evidence deepens as their ability to blend and surrender becomes stronger. Trance improves the flow, which improves all mediumship. The more out of the way and trusting of the energy we become, the better conduits for healing we are.

Trance is pure magic. It is a strong, tangible energy with deep connection and profound meaning.

13
Taking It Further

The journey with Spirit is always the journey *in*, rather than the journey *out*. You will face your own resistance to mediumship again and again. You may say to yourself:

- I am not good enough.
- If Spirit wanted me to do it they would make it easier.
- Who am I to do this job?
- I am not ready.
- I do not think I can do this.

What if that voice is never going to go away? What if it never stops? And what if it is not telling the truth? What if it is holding you back? Mediumship development is a mix of knowing when to take the leap and push yourself forward, and when to sit back and allow the lessons to integrate. I do not get this right all the time. All I can say is, where is that voice coming from? Is it your mind? If so, ignore it! If it is your heart or your gut, trust it. You have got this.

Your work now is not just to practice (practice plenty, please), but also to find out the medium you are, the medium you want to be. The greatest mediums I have ever seen work have reached a stage where they are comfortable with themselves and their mediumship. This is like being a child at the pic-n-mix counter. You have got to try it to work out which flavours you like! Do not be afraid to experiment with your style and how you want to work. Watch other mediums demonstrate. Go for readings. You will learn as much from what you like as from what you do not. Ask your questions of your Spirit guides. (e.g., Why does that medium do it like this? What does this mean?) The asking opens your valves and helps you to understand more and more about how this all works.

Allowing your unique style of mediumship is as important as the evidence you bring. The more you allow yourself to shine, the better that connection becomes.

Misinformation

There is a lot of confusing misinformation about the Spirit world spouted by mediums who have closed off their valves to alternative answers. I want to open you up to my understanding of Spirit in the hope this keeps your valves open and brings a new era of mediumship into being. Here are some examples:

- "Spirits get trapped here." They do not. Also, the Spirit world, with its infinite wisdom and power, most certainly do not need us to get involved with helping them cross over. What could I possibly bring to a trapped Spirit that an angel could not? We are experiencing and communicating with energy left behind from a life lived, not a soul.

- "A certain amount of time needs to pass before a reading." There is no time in the Spirit world, so the person who passed does not need time. I think it is more likely that the Spirit world will not communicate with a sitter if it will cause them damage or trauma. Timing has more do to with where the sitter is in their healing from loss, rather than the Spirit needing healing.

- "You can not communicate evidentially with someone the sitter has never met." Of course you can! Spirit are very clever! You will just need to be aware of different evidence, and make sure you keep those valves open. For example, I have had communications showing what the recipient has been up to that the Spirit has seen from the other side. One amazing lady showed me where she was on the family tree and a photograph that the recipient had with her for the event! Amazing!

- "The Spirit is too far away to communicate." I cannot imagine a Spirit wanting to make a communication with a loved one but standing just out of the medium's reach. I think this is a medium problem, not a Spirit one. If our energy is not in the right space so it can feel like they are just out of reach. Spirit are never difficult or obtuse. Although sometimes when they have felt far away to me, that has been evidential. For example, they lived overseas, they had another family, or they had a difficult relationship.

- "The wrong Spirit was sent." Again, Spirit are infinite wisdom and infinite love. They do not make mistakes. It can be embarrassing when the Spirit that shows up is not recognised or is not who the sitter wanted to hear from, but Spirit always know best. You will learn to trust over time, but please never bad mouth Spirit to a sitter. Show your faith and trust and it will only strengthen your connection. Most of the Spirits that have not been taken at one of my demonstrations are taken with 24 hours. People have all sorts of reasons for not being able to put their hand up at that moment, and your job is to allow them this experience however they can receive it.

Building Your Battery

It takes time and practice to be able to hold a Spirit connection. One of the things I never heard mediums talk about when I was developing is the cost to your physical self from doing this work. Over time I have realised that I have got stronger with more stamina, but that I have to accept there is a limit to what I can do and still do it well. Just like all mediumship, this depends on the individual so I cannot give you a specific guide, but I would suggest you allow yourself plenty of days off and lots of recovery time. I still need the following day to recover when I have done a demonstration to an audience, less so for a one-on-one reading.

Spirit show it to me like a battery. When you first start, you are an AA battery. You are drained in a reasonably short time, but it doesn't take you long to charge and recover. As you develop you will find your capacity to hold charge increases, you upgrade your battery again and again and again. You become a C battery, then a D, moving up to a car battery, ultimately as massive generator.

Then, your focus needs to be on ensuring you do not allow yourself to run completely flat. You know when your phone runs out and switches itself off? It takes longer to charge enough to get it turned back on. It is a much quicker process if you manage to catch it on 1%! Same for your mediumship battery. Try not to ever let yourself run completely empty and if you do, allow plenty of time to recover. Evidential mediumship is an altered state, this drains my battery far more quickly than psychic work does.

It is also important to have down times, when you are not trying to develop, expand or connect. As I have said before, you are here to be human not be a Spirit! Make sure you do not get so immersed in the Spirit world that you forget about the human one!

Ethics & Integrity

It is important as a representative of the Spirit world that you behave in a way that reflects their values and motivations. This does not mean become some version of yourself that you are not, but it is about questioning your behaviours and making sure they are coming from the right space. With the rise of the social media medium I have seen some things that have devastated me. For example, mediums asking for shares to allow Spirit to communicate, going up to people in a supermarket and giving them a reading without allowing them free will and choice in the matter, and the spreading of fear and the hierarchy of "I have a gift that you do not." Find your comfortable space and make sure that is what you communicate always. And question what you think all the time! It is the best way to make sure you are keeping those valves open to the way to be.

Language

Language is a human construct. The Spirit world does not need it. Spirit work with energy and intention. I have met a lot of people who believe that the words they hear are Spirit directly. But I do not think this is true. If that ability existed then mediums would be able to give messages in another language and mediumship demonstrations would not require interpreters! Even in trance, the Spirit world are communicating through our language. So, again, there is a part of us that remains present throughout.

This can mean that sometimes when you get a "no" it is not actually a "no". A massively overlooked idea in mediumship is to say the same thing again when you get a "no" but use different words. For example, I was once doing a reading for a man named Simon. I had his grandfather with me:

> Me: I have got a man here. He reaches retirement age but I know he passes sooner than he would have liked. He has a battle to stay. I believe he has cancer... lung cancer. Is this your grandfather?
>
> Simon: Yes.
>
> Me: I know he is a smartly dressed man, a professional, he works in an office and his job is about numbers.
>
> Simon: Yes.
>
> Me: He is a mischievous man.
>
> Simon: No.
>
> Me: (Going back to check with Spirit, still getting the same feeling, wondering what I am doing wrong.) He's naughty though, you remember this? He liked to play tricks on people and wind them up? He's like a school boy in a man's body?
>
> Simon: Oh yes, that is him alright!

Now to me, everything I said on my second attempt is still a man who is mischievous. But to Simon that word meant something else. Neither of us is right or wrong. This is the very nature of language and can be why sometimes we receive "no's" that are not actual wrong information at all! If when you get a "no" you still feel the same energy as you did, try another way with different words and see if that makes more sense to your sitter.

Energy Manifesting

Every word we speak creates a manifestation in our energy. If you start a reading saying things like:

- This is hard,
- I'm not in the right space to work,
- I can't do this, or
- I'm nervous,

you create more of that in your energy and your mediumistic experience. You can pinch yourself off from Spirit this way. I find the best space for me to work is a high energy one. As I mentioned earlier in the book, my favourite affirmation is as follows:

> *I am a phenomenal medium. I receive evidence with ease and clarity.*

I repeat that one to myself every day, many, many times. I say it to myself at least three times before I step out on stage.

When you are delivering information to your sitter be aware of your tone. Are you telling them or are you asking them? Asking creates more resistance in your energy! Even though it feels unnatural make sure you try to sound that you believe what you are saying, even when you are practising! Your energy will respond, which will increase your vibration and deepen your blend.

I also like to listen to music to get my blood pumping! I always told myself if I was truly Spiritual I should listen to Spiritual meditation music before work. How wrong I was! My best nights have been achieved by expanding my energy and warming up my throat rapping along to Eminem, Ru Paul, The Fugees and Iggy Azalea. It is not pretty and I am not sure I would like to share the experience with anyone else, but I always arrive at the venues ready to go! If you ever see me live you will hear us playing dance music and party classics to raise the vibration of the space.

On a recent retreat I hosted we had some students who were willing to try demonstrating to their peers. I asked them to meet me in the room fifteen minutes before the session started. Some of them were early and were attempting to meditate in preparation. The energy in the room was toxic! They were not meditating, they were panicking. Sitting in their fear. Focusing with worry on the task ahead. We put on Fatboy Slim and I made them all dance. We were crazy, jumping, whooping, leaping chucking shapes around the space like lunatics. And you know what? When the audience joined us, they got infected by the joy in that space! It was one of the best energies I have ever seen in a demonstration, and as a result the mediums all did brilliantly!

Do Not Take It All So Seriously!

Spirit work is important. It should be treated with respect and a sense of reverence. But it should still be fun. I know when I move into the Spirit world I will still want to laugh, to play and to be silly. The Spirits that work with you are exactly the same. Give yourself the gift of enjoying your mediumship and Spiritual practice. Play with the Spirit world.

One of my favourite things about demonstrating mediumship is the abundant, hilarious and unique personalities that come through to work with me, from the mother who wanted to complain her daughters had not looked after her grave to her impossibly high standards, to the grandmother who came through to offer her opinion about her grandaughter's new boyfriend and the big personality of the sister with breast cancer who made the nurses laugh and party while she was having chemo... it is so life affirming how normal the Spirits are, they do not become so watered down 'holy' version of a human, but rather keep those traits that made them who they were. And who they still continue to be.

Spirit are just happy to be with you. Happy for the chance to try. Happy to support you in your development.

Push Through

Here we are, at the end of the book, but the beginning of your journey. I hope this book has opened you up to the foundation of mediumship. Now you have that, it is time to build your own relationship with Spirit and discover the medium you want to be! It is my greatest wish that all developing mediums dedicate time to discovering who they are. Connect with what makes you, you. Fall in love with yourself. In the doing of this you will find your natural flow with your mediumship and the unique and wonderful medium you are. This is not about being the same as everyone else, it is about celebrating what makes you, you. Embrace your natural talents and personality and let that be your compass.

You will have days of doubts. Your fear will get in the way. That happens to us all. Just keep pushing through, striving, and being determined. Spirit always meets us much closer than halfway, you just have to take the step.

I know I am not the best medium in the world. There are others who have a greater capacity for evidence, who can commit to the surrender more than me, and who are more accomplished in their Spirit work. Spirit have taught me my "gift" is not limited to just mediumship. My gift is me: my ability to talk, my language, my personality. In embracing that, I have been lucky enough to attract so many of you to my teaching and my podcast. I am hoping that one day, when I have gone home to Spirit, I will feel proud of all the people I helped find the absolute joy in that connection for themselves.

You do not need to be a perfect medium to do the work and to help people. You just need to try. Keep shining your beautiful light, the world needs you more than you know.

Hannah x

Taking It Further Activities

Below are some more activities to expand your mediumship and take your practice further. When you have completed all of these, do not forget to ask Spirit to inspire you with some more!

Activity 16: Psychic Blending, Part 1 – Photographs

Ask a friend or family member for a photo of a loved one. Find a quiet space and allow your energy to settle. Move into the psychic frequency. I like to hold the photograph at the centre of my chest. Try not to look at the picture, try to *feel* the picture. What can you pick up about the person in the photograph? How were the feeling when it was taken? What kind of personality do they have? Can you feel any other information about them? Follow impressions, images and feelings you get and allow the energy to build.

Write down what you are getting. When you are done you can check what you got with the owner of the photograph!

You can also do this activity with objects, a practice known as psychometry. Hold the object in your hand and allow the impressions to unfold. Who owned this object? What can you tell about the people who have touched it? What is the object's history?

When you get comfortable with this practice, you can expand it. Start in the psychic frequency and move into the evidential mediumship. Use the object as an energetic key to call the prior owner to you and then start the blend with that spirit.

Activity 17: Psychic Blending, Part 2 – People

You need a willing volunteer for this one. Sit in front of your volunteer and allow your energy to become calm and still. Set your frequency to the psychic vibration. Send your energy out, imagine yourself expanding and wrapping your sitter up in your energy. As this blending takes place what do you experience from their energy? Try not to allow yourself to become limited by the ideas you have of things that will come up in a reading scenario. This is firstly about learning to perceive energy. Share all impressions you get, even random ones! Allow your sitter to tell you what makes sense to them and what does not.

This is such an important exercise for learn how to sit in both the energy of perception and the very human aspect of putting things you are feeling and perceiving into words. It makes you realise how much we hold in our energy, and how much information is available for us to experience and understand. I remember doing this activity with a group of students, someone felt like a right wally saying "bananas." But the sitter had spent the morning cutting up 20 of them to put in the freezer. It really is amazing what comes up!

Activity 18: Psychic Blending, Part 3 – Auragraphs

A fun way to work with energy and your psychic abilities is auragraphs. Auragraphs are a snapshot of someone's energy, both physical and nonphysical, using colour to get the information needed.

You will need a volunteer once more! Draw an outline of a human body on a piece pf A4 (8.5 x 11) paper. (There are lots of blank auragraphs online if you do a search). I prefer to use coloured pencils but felt tip pens work if you only have them. Sit in front of your sitter. Do not speak. You can play some nice meditation music if you want to fill the silence. Set your radio to the psychic frequency and settle your energy. As you tune into their energy what colour are you perceiving? Grab that colour pencil. Now, where do you feel that colour needs to be on this person's drawing? Start to colour. As you draw, surrender to the experience of that colour. Where do you want to draw it? What does it represent? How deep does the colour need to be? Why? Write down notes about what the colour means and where it is as you go, so you do not send your energy to your mind using your memory. When you have finished with that colour what colour is next? Repeat until you feel you are done (approximately 30 minutes). Fill the page! Colour over the lines! Keep questioning and asking about the energy you are receiving. You may have to fight your resistance – your brain will sometimes tell you, you are done way before you are, keep pushing through and seeking more.

When you are done share your findings with your sitter and allow yourself to bask in all the things you got right! Well done!

Activity 19: Sending Healing To A Plant Or Animal

You can send healing to a plant or animal easily and quickly. They do not have to be unwell. Healing can never cause damage. They will just take what they need and not absorb the rest. Animals have an unsettling way of moving in the energy and then getting up and removing themselves from it when they have had sufficient. Both animals and plants heal more quickly than humans, you will only be working for a few minutes.

Take a moment to settle your energy. Attune yourself to the healing frequency. Spend a moment focusing that energy on you. It is easy to rush in all guns blazing, but it's better to be slow and steady. Connect with healing energy through you first. When you feel settled and surrendered just direct that flow of healing to the plant or animal. Imagine it like a wave of light moving from you and surrounding the recipient. Allow it to flow. Be the vessel. Do not control or get in the way. When you feel that it is done allow it draw to a close and send out thanks to the Spirit world.

Activity 20: Ascended Masters

You can work with ascended masters to give you a different experience of the Spirit world, as well as access to their knowledge and teachings. You simply tune into the Spirit guide frequency and ask the relevant master to step forward. You can then ask them a question, or for some guidance. There are many ascended masters you can work with, but here are some ideas of ones to call on to get you started:

- Quan Yin, Goddess of compassion. I find her teachings gentle, kind-hearted and full of love.
- Saint Germaine. Saint Germaine brings magic, alchemy and transmutation. His guidance can help you to turn negatives into positives and invite more magic into your life. You can also ask him to bring forward the violet flame, an energy associated with change and the breaking of old patterns and beliefs.
- Kali, Goddess of Liberation and Rebirth. Call on Kali when you want change! She brings a strong, determined energy and will help you release the old to create the new.
- Lakshimi, Goddess of Abundance. Work with Lakshimi to break through those manifestation hurdles, to seek fulfilment and create a more comfortable material life.
- Jesus. Jesus brings strong love-centred teaching and guidance, alongside huge healing energy. His calm, funny and accessible personality have made him my all-time favourite ascended master to work with.

Activity 21: Archangels

When I work with angels, I can always feel the difference in their energy compared to my Spirit guides. They present to me as a higher vibration, which is easier to feel as it is more removed from my own. Archangels are angels who have reached a higher rank. Now, I am not sure about the human interpretation of hierarchies in the Spirit world. It seems a bit too much like life on Earth to me, but I still love to work with these energies and enjoy their teachings. Again, you just work in the Spirit guide frequency and ask the archangel you want to connect with to step forward. Here are a few to get you started:

- Archangel Michael brings protective energy, helps us to overcome fear, and be safe and secure in our unfoldment.
- Archangel Azrael assists with transition and support with grief.
- Archangel Chamuel brings strength to face challenges.
- Archangel Metatron brings healing, clearing of lower vibrational energies, and understanding of complex theological downloads from Spirit.
- Archangel Uriel. Call on Uriel if you feel stuck. He is also fab for learning and education and taking a practical approach to clearing emotions that might make us feel stuck, such as anger or fear.

Activity 22: Oracle Cards

I <u>love</u> oracle cards. I cannot get enough of them! The first rule of all oracles, whether they are pendulums, crystal balls, cards or anything else, is to always recognise you don't need them. Spirit are always communicating with you, and you have to find the balance between the fun and wonder of this objects and developing a reliance on them. If you have bought a set of oracle cards, I ask that you do not open the book that came with them! We can do better than that!

Start by settling your energy and powering up, working in the Spirit guide frequency. Ask to be guided to the message you need to hear. Pull a card (you can shuffle for a bit first if you want to). Which card have you got? What is the word or sentence written upon it? Look away from the card and focus on your Spirit guide beside you. What message do they have that relates to the card?

I recommend doing this often to strengthen the connection, but also mixing it up with the other activities listed. Do not get stuck on just one!

You can also use cards to:

- Answer a direct question (e.g., Should I move houses? How can I apply for that job? Where should I focus for my development next?)
- Give a "spread" reading. A spread is where you assign a value to each card and pull cards to fulfil that criteria. For example, a past, present, and future spread of three cards (one for each element). You can also do spreads for questions such as: What is available to me? What is preventing me from getting it? What action can I take?
- Direct your meditation.

- Channel a message for the collective, not just an individual.
- Have fun!!

I remember when I first started with cards, I had *The Answer is Simple* deck by Sonia Choquette. My friend and I were amazed by the accuracy of the answers we were receiving. My nonbelieving husband came home and we invited him to have a go. He pulled out two cards, one called "take your time" with a clock on it and one with "step away from the herd," covered in sheep. I asked him what he had wanted to know, and he laughed and said: "What was for dinner?" <u>The cards were right!</u> We were having slow cooked lamb. We laughed so hard.

Spirit are always willing to have as much fun with you as you will let them. If you remember to let joy lead the way, you will have the most fulfilling, exciting, and life-affirming journey ever!

I NEED YOUR HELP!

I am so incredibly grateful that you have purchased my book, and I hope it's given you all you need to start your journey with the Spirit world. If you can please take a moment to leave me a review I will be so happy, I know it's a boring job but it makes such a difference to budding writers to help get their work out there!

You can also get involved on social media by tagging me and using the hashtag #youareamedium for your posts – I would love to see you and how you're using the book, so don't be shy!

When you're ready to learn more do check out the Mediumship Matters podcast for further spiritual development guidance, plus the Mediumship Matters Spiritual School has a huge library of video lessons, exercises and live lessons to take your learning to the next level.

My website www.hannahmedium.co.uk has my books companion on it, created by my dear friend Kate, it cross references my podcast episodes and my school lessons so you can find out more about the subjects that light you up!

Acknowledgements

Mediumship is a difficult path. I love it, but it's a path I chose. Thank you to my family, who didn't choose this path, but were dragged along it by my obsession and wonder. Alex, Toby & Elodie, I love you.

Thank you to Jill Larking, Lynn Probert & Lynn Parker for helping my anxious, overanalytical, doubting self to take those first steps into mediumship.

Sue Q – the hours and hours we have spent, emptying restaurants with our zany conversations about spirit & development. I don't know what I'd have done without you. Thank you for being my sounding board, the voice of reason and an honourable comrade.

Thank you, Amanda, for always believing in me, I have no doubt I wouldn't have been brave enough to write this book without you. May you always know the power of your belief in others.

Thank you, Kim, for supporting me, always being honest and your faith in me – it always helps to know you are there, sending me supportive vibes and keeping the riff raff from the door!

Thank you, Jennifer Fezio, for bringing kindness and belief to me at my lowest development point. I'm not sure I'd have carried on without you. I am so grateful the Universe connected us from one side of the sea to the other. Looking forward to more together in the future!

To Lynn Gosney & Bruce Scott harbingers of my toughest lessons, bringers of the most necessary unfoldment. I owe so much of me to you. Thank you for holding a space that enabled me to be who I was meant to.

To all my students, listeners and followers – my greatest teachers. Thank you for sharing your stories, your questions and your experiences. It really is a collaborative experience, I am grateful to every single one of you x

*Available worldwide from Amazon
and all good bookstores*

Michael Terence Publishing

www.mtp.agency

mtp.agency

@mtp_agency

www.ingramcontent.com/pod-product-compliance
Lightning Source LLC
LaVergne TN
LVHW051218070526
838200LV00064B/4961